PRAISE FOR *THE HOPE QUOTIENT*

"Ray is one of our great Christian communicators. What the world needs is hope, the hope of Jesus Christ. Thank you, Ray, for helping us raise our Hope Quotient."

—MARK BURNETT
PRODUCER, *SON OF GOD* MOVIE

"I have known Ray Johnston for many years, and if anyone exudes the true nature and reality of hope, it's Ray! You see it in his walk with God, in his family life, and in the life of his church. In this book, Ray reveals how enthusiasm, fresh vision, creativity, and determination all come from hope. I have no doubt the wisdom found in this book will bless many. It did me!"

—LUIS PALAU
EVANGELIST AND AUTHOR, *OUT OF THE
DESERT...INTO THE LIFE GOD FULLY INTENDED*

"If you are discouraged, down, or disheartened, Ray Johnston's book *The Hope Quotient* is just what you need. This book will build your faith, give you strength to move forward, and help you overcome the challenges before you. Sometimes all you need is a little hope."

—CRAIG GROESCHEL
SENIOR PASTOR, LIFECHURCH.TV
AUTHOR, *FIGHT*

"If I were to recommend one book to you it would be *The Hope Quotient* by Pastor Ray Johnston. Being in ministry I can tell you that life leaves most of us feeling drained, out of balance, and without hope. *The Hope Quotient* gives you everything you need to refill your tank, engage life, and put God's hope back in your heart. Read it, enjoy it, and pass it on."

—MIKE NOVAK
PRESIDENT AND CEO, KLOVE AND AIRI

"We've heard a lot about Intelligence Quotient (IQ) and Emotional Intelligence (EQ), but Ray Johnston makes a compelling case that the most important factor of all may be our Hope Quotient (HQ). He reminds us, along with the apostle Paul, that 'hope does not disappoint, because the love of God has been poured out within our hearts through the Holy Spirit who was given to us' (Rom. 5:5 NASB)."

—JIM DALY
PRESIDENT, FOCUS ON THE FAMILY

"Ray Johnston is a high energy, life-giving, people-building hope machine. I am so glad he's passing some of his secrets on for you and me."

—JOHN ORTBERG
SENIOR PASTOR, MENLO PARK PRESBYTERIAN CHURCH
AUTHOR, *WHO IS THIS MAN?*

"Ray Johnston is an incredible pastor and leader. He's learned these lessons over many years of faithfully following Christ and serving others. I'm so thankful he's sharing these powerful insights with all of us!"

—JUD WILHITE
SENIOR PASTOR, CENTRAL CHRISTIAN CHURCH
AUTHOR, *THE GOD OF YES*

"If hope were a person, it would be Ray Johnston! He exudes life, passion, and amazing energy at all times. I know *The Hope Quotient* will give meaning and significance to so many looking for a hope-filled life. I dare you to read this book without walking away inspired and ready to change the world!"

—BRAD LOMENICK
PAST PRESIDENT AND KEY VISIONARY, CATALYST
AUTHOR, *THE CATALYST LEADER*

"Not only is Ray one of my closest friends, he is also a man I have had the pleasure of learning from and serving with for the last fourteen years. Ray believes the things that he's written in this book so much that he lives this book! I can't wait to hear the stories of lives renewed and recharged as a result of people raising their HQ!"

—LINCOLN BREWSTER
WORSHIP PASTOR, BAYSIDE CHURCH
INTEGRITY MUSIC RECORDING ARTIST

"Ray Johnston has more energy and creativity than ten men. But after reading this book, I think he has more hope as well . . . and you can too."

—DAVE STONE
SOUTHEAST CHRISTIAN, LOUISVILLE, KENTUCKY

"I like Ray Johnston because he has great faith in God and puts it into action in his church and in his life. Out of his faith comes hope, the purpose of this book. I pray that God will use this message of hope to motivate the hopeless, to kick start the apathetic, to enliven those who've had life crushed out of them. Great book, Ray. May God use it in great ways."

—ELMER TOWNS
COFOUNDER, LIBERTY UNIVERSITY

"This book is exactly like Ray Johnston—inspirational and encouraging. For those who have hope, HQ will no doubt give you more. For those who need hope, HQ will show you how. This book has moved inside my top ten inspirational books of all time."

—JIM BURNS, PHD
PRESIDENT, HOMEWORD
AUTHOR, *CREATING AN INTIMATE MARRIAGE* AND *CONFIDENT PARENTING*

"*The Hope Quotient* is what every leader needs to take their influence to the next level! Readers be warned, you will soon discover you are not reading this book . . . it's reading you!"

—BIL CORNELIUS
FOUNDING PASTOR, BAY AREA FELLOWSHIP
AUTHOR, *TODAY IS THE DAY*

"In the following pages Ray Johnston unleashes the hidden power of hope in a way that will change your life forever. This book will reignite your passion for dreaming big and stepping into the fullness of all God has for you. You're going to be hard pressed to find a book with more motivation or inspiration. Ray doesn't just teach about hope; he embodies it. This is a must-read."

—MARGARET FEINBERG
AUTHOR, *WONDERSTRUCK*

"Hope matters. Big time. Ray Johnston has written an incredibly helpful book that moves beyond the happy talk of motivation clichés to real-life, feet-on-the-ground, practical advice for raising our HQ (Hope Quotient) and changing the way we perceive and experience the world around us. Read it. You'll be glad you did."

—LARRY OSBORNE
AUTHOR AND PASTOR,
NORTH COAST CHURCH, VISTA, CA

"If there was ever a person who qualified as a human dynamo, it's my friend Ray Johnston. Thank God he focuses his boundless energy on his wife, his kids, his church, his messages, and now, this fabulous manuscript. Be forewarned, Ray's enthusiasm is contagious. It won't take long before we're all talking about HQ."

—BILL BUTTERWORTH
SPEAKER AND AUTHOR, *BALANCING
WORK AND LIFE* AND *THE SHORT LIST*

"Hope is one of God's essential fuels for the soul. In this book, Ray pours hope into a spectrometer to understand its chemical makeup. These are not hackneyed pointers for wishful thinking; these are substantive principles for empowered living."

—REV. GARY WALTER
PRESIDENT, THE EVANGELICAL
COVENANT CHURCH

"If you have been around Ray for more than ten minutes, then you have been encouraged and given hope. It's no surprise then that this newest book comes from the core of who he is, and shares some practical steps for how the rest of us can live a life filled with hope as well. This is a must-read for those who struggle with feelings of doubt, defeat, and the ugly effects of pessimism."

—CHRIS BROWN
CO-SENIOR PASTOR AND TEACHING
PASTOR, NORTH COAST CHURCH

"Having grown up as a poor street kid in the most difficult parts of Uganda, I can truly say that hope is what kept me going in the midst of what felt like endless darkness. Hope is what kept me thriving when it made no sense, and ultimately, what allowed me to be rescued from my hopelessness and put on a path toward a better life. In this book, Ray has done a great job unpacking ways in which you can live every moment of every day with inescapable hope, spurring us on to be generous with our families, workplaces, local communities, and people all over world who need a little hope."

—PETER HABYARIMANA
CHURCH ENGAGEMENT, COMPASSION INTERNATIONAL

"I have known Ray Johnston for more than thirty years and consider *The Hope Quotient* one of the most significant contributions available to anyone looking for more in life. This is a must-read for everyone regardless of age, beliefs, or circumstances. His seven essentials will revolutionize your life and raise your Hope Quotient. His book is a gracious gift to you, the reader."

—JON R. WALLACE
PRESIDENT, AZUSA PACIFIC UNIVERSITY

"My friend Ray Johnston has written *the* book on hope. *The Hope Quotient* is the core of his soul, and as a fellow traveler and leader in life, I want you to know Ray lives these principles out in his life and ministry. Read *The Hope Quotient* and transform your life!"

—DR. JOHN JACKSON
AUTHOR AND PRESIDENT, WILLIAM JESSUP UNIVERSITY

"The book is for *everyone* who desires more hope in their lives through what Pastor Ray preaches and practices: a deeper relationship with Jesus Christ, our ultimate hope. Measure Him and raise Him and you will never be the same."

—CHRISTIAN OGOEGBUNEM ISICHEI, MD
FOUNDING COORDINATOR, FAITH ALIVE FOUNDATION, NIGERIA
PROFESSOR AND CONSULTANT CHEMICAL PATHOLOGIST,
UNIVERSITY OF JOS/JOS UNIVERSITY TEACHING HOSPITAL,
JOS, NIGERIA

"I will read anything and everything Ray puts in print! He is a tremendous author because he's a tremendous person and leader! He's right-on with his thoughts."

—CLARK MITCHELL
FOUNDING SENIOR PASTOR,
JOURNEYCHURCH.TV

"Ray Johnston is one of the most effective pastoral leaders in America, having built an innovative and effective congregation, Bayside Church in Sacramento. He speaks and writes in an incredibly engaging way. Ray is a gift to the American church and his voice an important one for this moment in American church history."

—DR. MAC PIER
CEO AND FOUNDER,
THE NEW YORK CITY LEADERSHIP CENTER

"Hope tends to be an elusive thought, but Ray has brought it down to where it can be lived, understood, and experienced so we can become the people God intended for us to be when we were born."

—JO ANNE LYON
GENERAL SUPERINTENDENT, THE WESLEYAN CHURCH

"As a life fitness coach I see firsthand everyday the connection between the physical, emotional, and mental. Pastor Ray has taken hope and has boiled it down to irreducible minimums so that if a person will take the information in this book and apply it on a regular basis, it will result in sustainable transformation in key areas of their life."

—DON NAVA
LIFE FITNESS COACH, THE TOTALLY FIT LIFE

"Pastor Ray has a higher Hope Quotient than anyone I know. He is a world-class guy, speaker, father, and friend. In this book, he offers simple, practical advice so the rest of us can start moving our HQ in Ray's direction. He mixes in his trademark stories so the book is even a breeze to read. No one needs to hope this book will be a raging success; it will be."

—PAUL CARROLL
SEVENTEEN-YEAR VETERAN REPORTER AND
EDITOR, *WALL STREET JOURNAL*
AUTHOR, *THE NEW KILLER APPS* AND *BIG BLUES*

"Hopelessness and discouragement are thumbs on the throat of the world, slowly choking people to death. In *The Hope Quotient*, Ray Johnston shows us how to release the death grip of negativity and launch into a new freshness of life—a place where we breathe deeply, live clearly, and achieve the dreams in our hearts. Thank you, Ray, for showing us how to be free of the death grip of hopelessness and for setting us on a path full of hope."

—PAUL COLE
PRESIDENT, CHRISTIAN MEN'S NETWORK

"Ray Johnston's *The Hope Quotient* will guide you to become a person filled with hope, which will enable you to live more fully, driven by vision and expectancy. That will impact your relationships, your professional life, your accomplishments, and your sense of satisfaction and contentment. Your Hope Quotient will have a profound impact on how you live your life."

—PAUL FRIESEN
AUTHOR, *THE MARRIAGE APP*

"Ray Johnston is the most encouraging person I know. He absolutely radiates confidence in God. In *The Hope Quotient*, Ray introduces you to other powerfully hope-filled people whose amazing stories will cause your hope level to rocket to new heights! Best of all, when you finish *The Hope Quotient*, you'll be an agent of hope too. Read this. Read it because you need a dose of hope—and read it because your friends and family need you to activate the power of hope in their own lives."

—RENE SCHLAEPFER
PASTOR, TWIN LAKES CHURCH
AUTHOR, *GRACE IMMERSION* AND *JESUS JOURNEY*

THE HOPE QUOTIENT

HQ

THE HOPE QUOTIENT

HQ

Measure It. Raise It.
You'll Never Be the Same.

RAY JOHNSTON

W PUBLISHING GROUP

AN IMPRINT OF THOMAS NELSON

Published in Nashville, Tennessee, by W Publishing, an imprint of Thomas Nelson.

Author is represented by the literary agency of Alive Communications, Inc., 7680 Goddard Street, Suite 200, Colorado Springs, CO 80920, www.alivecommunications.com.

Illustrations by Jason Gregory

Stock images p#/artist © Shutterstock: 1/Dionisvera, 143/pzAxe

Thomas Nelson titles may be purchased in bulk for educational, business, fund-raising, or sales promotional use. For information, please e-mail SpecialMarkets@ThomasNelson.com.

Any Internet addresses, phone numbers, or company or product information printed in this book are offered as a resource and are not intended in any way to be or to imply an endorsement by Thomas Nelson, nor does Thomas Nelson vouch for the existence, content, or services of these sites, phone numbers, companies, or products beyond the life of this book.

Every effort has been made to identify and trace copyright holders and to obtain their permission for the use of copyrighted material. The publisher apologizes for any errors or omissions and would be grateful if notified of any corrections that should be incorporated in future reprints or editions of this book.

Unless otherwise noted, Scripture quotations are taken from the Holy Bible, New International Version®, NIV®. Copyright © 1973, 1978, 1984, 2011 by Biblica, Inc.™ Used by permission of Zondervan. All rights reserved worldwide. www.zondervan.com. Scripture quotations marked AMP are taken from the Amplified® Bible. Copyright © 1954, 1958, 1962, 1964, 1965, 1987 by The Lockman Foundation. Used by permission. (www.Lockman.org). Scripture quotations marked CEV are taken from the Contemporary English Version. Copyright © 1991, 1992, 1995 by the American Bible Society. Used by permission. Scripture quotations marked ESV are taken from The Holy Bible, English Standard Version® (ESV®), copyright © 2001 by Crossway, a publishing ministry of Good News Publishers. Used by permission. All rights reserved. Scripture quotations marked GNT are taken from the Good News Translation in Today's English Version—Second Edition. Copyright 1992 by American Bible Society. Used by permission. Scripture quotations marked KJV are taken from the King James Version (public domain). Scripture quotations marked NASB are taken from New American Standard Bible®, Copyright © 1960, 1962, 1963, 1968, 1971, 1972, 1973, 1975, 1977, 1995 by The Lockman Foundation. Used by permission. (www.Lockman.org). Scripture quotations marked NKJV are taken from the New King James Version®. © 1982 by Thomas Nelson, Inc. Used by permission. All rights reserved. Scripture quotations marked NLT are taken from the Holy Bible, New Living Translation. © 1996, 2004, 2007. Used by permission of Tyndale House Publishers, Inc., Carol Stream, Illinois 60188. All rights reserved.

Library of Congress Control Number: 2014930317

ISBN: 978-0-52910-115-0

ISBN: 978-0-71801-152-9 (ITPE)

Printed in the United States of America

18 19 20 21 LSC 10 9 8 7 6 5 4 3

To my wife, Carol

It isn't often in life that someone gets his first choice and it turns out even better than he hoped. For the last thirty years you have loved me, loved our four kids, and loved the people God has called us to lead. You continue to be the best example of hope I have ever seen. I will be forever grateful that I am married to the person that I respect most in the world. Thirty years . . . a pretty good start!

May the God of hope fill you with all joy and peace as you trust in him, so that you may overflow with hope by the power of the Holy Spirit.

ROMANS 15:13

CONTENTS

READ THIS FIRST

Tough circumstances are no match for the kind of inner strength fueled by hope.

- Lock him in a prison cell, beat him, and shipwreck him, and you have the apostle Paul.
- Deafen him, and you have a Ludwig van Beethoven.
- Cripple him, and you have a brilliant novelist and poet—Sir Walter Scott.
- Raise him in abject poverty, and you have an Abraham Lincoln.
- Burn him so severely that doctors say he'll never walk again, and you have a Glenn Cunningham—the man who set the world's one-mile record in 1934.
- Strike him down with infantile paralysis, and he becomes a Franklin D. Roosevelt.
- Call him a slow learner, label him "retarded," and write him off as uneducable, and you have an Albert Einstein.
- Have her born black in a society filled with racial discrimination, and you have a Rosa Parks.
- Subject him to torture in a Japanese prison camp for more than three years, and you have a Louis Zamperini.

READ THIS SECOND

(Don't Worry, the Book Will Start Soon)

Once in a great while, a book comes along that changes how everybody thinks. That happened in 1995 when Daniel Goleman released his book *Emotional Intelligence: Why It Can Matter More than IQ.*[1] Goleman hit the nail with his head! He accurately described something that deep inside we all knew was true—some very smart people don't do well in life because they don't have a clue how to relate to people. For the last twenty years, people have understood that someone's EQ (Emotional Intelligence Quotient) is as important to success in life and relationships as their IQ (Intelligence Quotient).

Great book—brilliant idea! It just didn't go far enough.

I've been a professor, pastor, coach, husband, and dad (by far the hardest job), and I'm currently president of Thrive Communications, which means that every year I'm face-to-face with more than four hundred thousand people in some context. (Whew, I'm getting tired just writing this!) Every day I have the privilege of working with a broad cross-section of accomplished people—everyone from CEOs to soccer moms. And this is what I've observed: IQ and EQ are not enough.

Let me pose some simple questions. Why are some people more effective than other people? Why do some enjoy life while others endure life? Why do some soar while others sink? Consider some specific scenarios, because it's the same in every area of life. Why are some marriages closer? Why do some parents get more out of parenting? Why do some businesspeople advance in their careers while others plateau? Why do some people thrive emotionally, seem more happy, more fulfilled? In short, *why are some people just personally, emotionally, and relationally in better shape?*

Let me give you the whole book in one sentence: thriving people thrive for one reason—they commit to things that produce inner strength and hope.

And here's the good news. *Unlike IQ and EQ, which are largely inherited, your degree of hope, your "Hope Quotient" or HQ, can be developed to any level.*

I have invested seven years into researching and writing this book (with real people, not rats!), and it has been worth every second. In fact, what I have discovered is so important that my team has developed an online assessment tool, just for you, which I'll tell you about in a few chapters.

It all started with a simple conversation with my daughter . . .

PART ONE

THE SINGLE MOST IMPORTANT THING TO DO

1.

WHERE IT BEGAN

Some conversations change your life. You just don't expect them to be with one of your kids.

Several years ago, my daughter Leslie came home from school and said, "Dad, I have to write a paper on a leader."

"Yeah?" I said.

"I picked you, and the teacher said it was okay," she said.

"*Yeah . . . ,*" I said, growing wary.

Without hesitating, she laid it out before me. "I have twenty questions. This is going to be at least a two-hour interview, and you have to answer them all honestly."

At that, we grabbed our swimsuits and hopped into the hot tub. I thought, *Since I'm going to end up in hot water anyway, I might as well start there!*

Two hours later, she asked me her last question. It caught me by surprise. Her last question was her best question. And her last question was one of the most profound questions that human beings can ever ask themselves.

"What's the single most important thing you do as a leader?"

I looked at her and said, "That's easy. The single most important thing I do is make sure I stay encouraged."

She looked at me with this blank stare—kind of like, *what?* Just as you may be looking at this book right now. I explained it to her.

"If I'm not encouraged, eventually nothing else matters.

"If I'm not encouraged, I'll never be the communicator people who listen to me need me to be.

"If I'm not encouraged, I'll never be the person I believe God wants me to be."

I got a little choked up, looked at Leslie, and said, "If I'm not encouraged, I will never be the dad you need me to be.

"If I'm not encouraged, I'll never be the husband Mom dreams I *might* be someday." (Married guys know *exactly* what I'm talking about.)

Why is this a big deal? Because getting and staying encouraged is everyone's number one need—whether they know it or not.

Let me tell you about my day yesterday. I met for an hour and a half with some great people, leaders of a local chain of restaurants. They brought me in to train their executives and employees. What was their number one need? Fresh vision for the future. Where does that come from? Hope.

That was followed by a telephone conversation with an attorney friend from Southern California. He's a sharp guy and a strong Christian, but his heart is breaking because his son has turned away from his family's faith and values and is taking some destructive paths. What was that dad's number one need? He needs the kind of inner strength that only comes to people who have hope.

I then did a Livestream video seminar with leaders from all over the country on how to turn a church from stagnant and declining to thriving. What was the number one need of the leaders of these churches? The kind of creativity and determination that only comes to people who have hope.

I stopped at a gas station and talked with a twenty-four-year-old college dropout who just came back to our area. As we put gas in our cars (a very expensive proposition), he told me he was out of work. What was his number one need? The kind of focus and resolve that only comes to people who have hope.

I wrapped up my day and was driving out of our church parking lot when I saw a poised, professional woman who looked lost. She said she was searching for one of the conference rooms. I asked her which meeting she was attending.

She hesitated, embarrassed, then said the DivorceCare seminar. My heart immediately went out to her. I got out of my car and walked her to her class. She turned to me before she walked through the door, and I saw tears streaming down her face. She said, "It's just really hard." What is her number one need? Hope. I touched her shoulder and said, "God has better days ahead."

Think about the opposite. Howard Hendricks gave a gripping definition of discouragement: "Discouragement is the anesthetic the devil uses on a person just before he reaches in and carves out his heart."[1] He's right. When people lose hope, they lose their ability to dream for the future. Despair replaces joy. Fear replaces faith. Anxiety replaces prayer. Insecurity replaces confidence. Tomorrow's dreams are replaced by nightmares. It's a lousy way to live.

When spouses lose hope, they give up on their marriages. Parents give up on their teens. Leaders give up on their people. Healthy emotions like contentment and peace are replaced with the toxic emotions of confusion, shame, worry, and disappointment. In short, it's impossible to be spiritually, psychologically, emotionally, or relationally healthy when we're gripped by discouragement.

Some wise person once said that we can live about forty days without food, about three days without water, about eight minutes without air—but not a single second without hope. And that is why . . .

- the greatest gift leaders can give their people—*hope.*
- the greatest gift parents can give their children—*hope.*
- the greatest gift teachers can give their students—*hope.*
- the greatest gift coaches can give their athletes—*hope.*

It's also why . . .

- the greatest gift *you* can give your family—hope.
- the greatest gift *you* can give your friends—hope.
- the greatest gift *you* can give your neighbors—hope.
- the greatest gift *you* can give your coworkers—hope.

The truth is, the greatest gift you or I can give *anyone* is hope.

Think hope doesn't make a difference? Let's get real for a second. Two people are walking in your direction. One of them is the most *encouraging* person you know. The other is the most *discouraging* person you know. Which one do you want to spend time with? That is true in every setting.

In fact, picture what happens when a person of genuine hope comes into your life. All it takes is one. In a flash, the whole atmosphere changes. The impossible actually starts to look possible (think Steve Jobs). Defeat starts to look like it could be turned to victory (think Peyton Manning). Difficult things begin to look like they might actually be possible (think Nelson Mandela). Courage replaces fear, and strength chases away powerlessness.

Yes, hope is *that* important!

Imagine two lives with identical circumstances, except one person faces those circumstances with hope and confidence, and the other person does not. How differently would those two lives turn out from one another?

My observation after working with leaders around the world is that these hold true. The presence of hope and confidence creates *eleven* major differences. You will

- have more satisfying relationships,
- be more productive,
- be less affected by stress,
- be more successful,
- feel more satisfied,
- be more compassionate,
- be more willing to help people in need,
- be physically healthier,
- hold to higher moral and ethical standards,
- be more likely to assume leadership, and
- be more likely to see God as loving, caring, and forgiving.

Do you realize that rising hope can change everything for you too? Regardless of your background, regardless of your job, regardless of your personal makeup or life history, the priority of staying encouraged *by learning how to increase your Hope Quotient* can change everything.

But let me give one caution here. If you came to this book looking for a typical, shallow, self-help book with catchy phrases that don't work, then you picked up the wrong title. Too many books that promise hope end up giving little more than pious platitudes and anemic answers. Hope can seem like cotton candy, which tastes good at first, but there's nothing to it. *Real hope is a deep and powerful force when it is anchored in the seven factors that sustain hope.*

The *last* thing anybody needs is a shot of hope, a temporary high followed by a crash. On January 1, people get a temporary shot of hope and set New Year's resolutions, and by January 6 they're done with them. People get a temporary shot of hope, decide they're going to lose weight, and three pounds later, give up. Countless people have said, "This is the year I'm going to read the Bible," and then make it all the way to Genesis 6. The common denominator in these situations is a temporary, emotional, shallow burst of hope not anchored in the seven factors that support, sustain, and strengthen hope.

This book, and the online test you can take with it, will help you build the seven factors of your life that will help you not just *get* encouraged but *stay* encouraged. This is the battle you want to win and the one battle you cannot afford to lose.

2.

YOUR HQ CHANGES EVERYTHING

Be strong and let your heart take courage,
All you who hope *in the* LORD.

PSALM 31:24 NASB; EMPHASIS ADDED

When you say a situation or a person is hopeless, you are
slamming the door in the face of God.

CHARLES L. ALLEN

I walked out of his house in the hills above Hollywood, telephoned my wife, and said, "I have just met the greatest single human being I will ever meet." His name is Louis Zamperini. At age ninety-six, he is also one of the most energetic.

I had just spent four hours interviewing him on camera in the home he has owned for over sixty years—a home too little for a life lived so large. Each tabletop and corner was crammed with memories and tributes—everything from the five Olympic torches he had carried, including a torch he carried out of the Japanese POW camp where he had been held as a prisoner during World War II; to the trophies commemorating his athletic achievements; to picture upon picture of him with Hollywood celebrities; to a birthday card he had received a month earlier from Billy Graham. Great guy, great sense of humor—which is *amazing* considering everything he has gone through.

Credit: CJ Alvarado

I first read the unforgettable story of Louie's trip to hell and back in Laura Hillenbrand's runaway bestseller *Unbroken*, which, by the way, is a great read.[1] Louie's life story could be described with three words: *it gets worse.*

Louie ran for the United States in the 1936 Olympic Games in Berlin. He told me he met Hitler personally and that, in an instant, he didn't like him. He even showed me the Nazi flag he stole and brought back. He ran so well in Berlin that he was favored to win in the next Olympics. Experts thought he had a good chance to become the first runner to break the four-minute mile barrier, but the outbreak of World War II derailed those dreams. Louie instead joined the Army Air Corps, becoming a lieutenant and serving as a bombardier. In May 1943, his plane crashed into the Pacific Ocean.

Louie survived. Then things got worse.

For more than a month, with no food or water, Louie and the two other survivors, baked by the sun during the day and frozen by the cold ocean air at night, drifted west some two thousand miles on a pair of fading canvas rafts. Above them blazed a merciless, blistering sun, while below them flashed the sharp teeth of circling sharks. After battling the sea, storms, sharks, and starvation, they miraculously hit land. They were near death when they were captured and sent to a place known as Execution Island, where every known prisoner had been put to death.

That's where the real nightmare began.

Torture, hours of beatings, raging thirst, emaciation, maggots, mosquitoes, rats, humiliation, loneliness, interrogations, experimentations, a total loss of dignity—all this caused Louie to look at himself and think, *All I see is a dead body breathing.* He hoped for better treatment when his captors unexpectedly transferred him to a Yokohama POW camp, but again things got worse. He soon found out he'd landed instead at a secret interrogation center. It meant an even more severe round of beatings, mutilations, starvation, diarrhea, lice, fleas, slave labor, and executions. Eventually, Louie got transferred again. Reflecting on those days, Louie remarked, "If I knew I had to go through those experiences again, I'd kill myself."[2]

And then it got worse—just when it looked like it was getting better.

Louie's prison camp was liberated by the Allies. In America newspaper headlines had already mourned his death, and his family even held a funeral. Louie became like someone resurrected from the dead. He came home to the embrace of his shocked family and a hero's welcome—parades, Hollywood stars. But while the war years were gone, they were anything but forgotten. Louie was a celebrity, but inside he was a mess. Haunted by nightmares, he turned to alcohol for relief. As Louie told me, "Nobody back then had ever heard of post-traumatic stress disorder."[3]

For the first five years of his post-POW life, homicidal hatred toward his captors consumed him. Determination, a hardy body, and maybe pure spite had kept him alive throughout his captivity, but nothing in him could prevent his free fall into despair once he returned home.

Yet Louis Zamperini *didn't* slide into the abyss. What stopped him? I asked him. His answer, in a word, was *hope.* Louie's wife, in a last-ditch effort to save their marriage, dragged him to a Billy Graham crusade. That night Billy spoke words Louie didn't want to hear and felt determined to disbelieve.

Over the course of two nights, everything changed. After the second night, Louie went home and walked over to the liquor cabinet. His wife looked at him with an *Oh no, it didn't work* look. He opened the cabinet, took out every bit of alcohol in it, went into the kitchen, and poured it all down the sink. He threw all the bottles into the trash. He hasn't had a drink of alcohol ever since. That night, for the first time since his liberation, the nightmares didn't come. The following morning,

> Louie felt profound peace. When he thought of his history, what resonated with him now was not all that he had suffered but the divine love that he believed had intervened to save him. . . . In a single, silent moment, his rage, his fear, his humiliation and helplessness, had fallen away. That morning, he believed, he was a new creation.[4]

Infused with a new energy—Hillenbrand calls Louie "infectiously effervescent and apparently immortal"[5]—he founded a boys' camp, embarked on a worldwide speaking tour, carried the Olympic torch at five different Games, regularly ran a six-minute mile in his sixties, began skateboarding in his seventies, and in his nineties was still climbing trees that needed pruning. In Laura Hillenbrand's words, he "remained infectiously, incorrigibly cheerful."[6] In my words, *the guy is still a riot!*

As we were leaving, Louie stopped me and said, "I forgot to tell you my best story!"

We turned the cameras back on, and he said, "During the Nagano Olympics, I was invited to speak in the Sugamo prison—the same prison where I was tortured. The mayor gathered most of the town and held a press conference question-and-answer with the two of us for about an hour. When the time came for the last question, I could tell that the mayor was embarrassed to ask it. He finally cleared his throat and said, 'Um, Louie, this may be a hard question to answer but I want to ask. Did anything positive result in your life as a result of being in a Japanese prisoner of war camp for two years?'"

Louie told me that he smiled and said, "Yes, being in a prisoner of war camp for two years prepared me for fifty years of marriage."[7] I almost fell off the couch!

I walked out of Louie's house with a profound appreciation for the power of hope. It was hope that liberated Louie from discouragement, despair, and potential suicide. It was hope that kept him alive in a concentration camp. It was hope that replaced hatred with forgiveness. It was hope that, during the worst circumstances imaginable, allowed him to remain "unbroken." And it is that kind of fresh hope that continues to make Louis Zamperini one of the most delightful, fun, joyful, and resilient people on the planet.

Does hope *really* have that kind of power, or is Louie's experience a one-shot deal? I'm convinced that with the smallest increase in hope, *anything* is possible.

The 10 Percent Solution

A few years ago, I had the privilege of meeting with a leading psychologist who told me something amazing. He had built his career around working with deeply troubled married couples who had been damaging their relationships for decades. He enjoyed remarkable success in getting these warring spouses to turn the corner toward health. Counseling is not my greatest gift, so his obvious skill sparked my curiosity. How did he do it?

"I just try to get 10 percent improvement," he said. "When couples get that 10 percent improvement, they get hope. *And when someone gets hope, anything is possible.*"

It's an amazing thought. When a struggling individual gets just a 10 percent boost in hope, almost anything becomes possible. I looked back over my life and realized that I've seen a 10 percent rise in hope transform horrendous situations into amazingly *great* ones.

Hope is so potent that you don't need to get 50 percent more hopeful, or 40 percent, or even 25 percent. Just 10 percent more hope is enough to launch you into a new and better orbit.

> ## That makes hope the highest-octane fuel in the universe.

When you get 10 percent improvement, you get a higher Hope Quotient. And when your HQ is high, anything's possible. Hope is the beginning of *everything*.

- When people become more hopeful about their health, they start on the path to getting in shape.
- When people get hopeful about breaking bad habits, they start winning battles they haven't won before.
- When people become more hopeful about their kids, they find new energy to invest in those kids.
- When people get hope in their marriages, they start making better decisions.
- When people become more hopeful about their finances, they begin to develop the patterns that lead to financial freedom.
- When people become more hopeful about their future, hope is the match that lights the fuse that sends them back to school or helps them apply for a new job or helps them grow and develop.
- When people become more hopeful that they can actually connect with God, it fuels the kind of actions that lead them to spiritual vitality and health.

Hope is *the* most important factor, because when you have hope, anything is possible. I'm convinced that any great thing that ever happens in your life, in your family, in your marriage, in your community, in your country, and in your world happens because someone has achieved a higher hope level.

Hope will do four things for you that *nothing* else can do.

Four Things Hope Does That Nothing Else Can Do

Of all the remarkable things I've seen hope do in my life and in the lives of others, these four things stand out:

1. Hope liberates. *Hope releases you from your past.*
2. Hope motivates. *Hope helps you bounce back.*
3. Hope initiates. *Hope sets you free to dream.*
4. Hope activates. *Hope is the fuel that makes the world a better place.*

Let's take a quick look at each of these, because I want you to see the enormous life change that genuine hope can bring both to you and to our hope-starved world.

1. Hope liberates. Hope releases you from your past.

What kept Louis Zamperini from plunging off the cliff? There were several he could have gone over. Hope stopped his fall. Hope liberates people from the chains that imprison them. It sets them free from past failures and hurts, dysfunctional family patterns, guilt, low expectations, and even crippling lack of confidence.

I grew up in something of an executive, jet-set family, where divorce ruled. *Everybody* got divorced. We cannot find a lasting marriage in 150 years of our family tree. Add to that my family's raging alcoholism and explosive anger, and maybe you can see why divorce was epidemic and how I grew up convinced that my life probably wouldn't feature a lasting marriage. At no time did I ever think, *I can have a fulfilling family life.*

That belief got a major makeover after a bunch of terrific couples put their arms around me in an awesome Southern California church of 110 people. For the first time in my life, I saw couples that had been married for ten, fifteen, twenty, and even thirty or more years. During five years in that church, I never saw a single couple break up. That totally changed my frame of reference. For the first time, I thought, *Wow! I could really have a lasting marriage. That could be* my *future.*

My wife, Carol, and I just celebrated our thirtieth anniversary, which means I am in the longest-lasting marriage in the history of my family. We have four children—Mark, Scott, Christy, and Leslie—whom, as of the date of this writing, I still like, and who, more amazingly, like *me.* They are incredible young adults who love Jesus and who look forward to one day creating their own strong marriages and loving families. Thirty years ago, I couldn't imagine any of this.

The couples in that church gave me a great gift. They liberated me from the expectation that my past background would be the determining factor in my future relationships. Hope will do that for you. Hope liberates from past failures, from bitterness, from anger, from insecurity, and from the kind of low expectations that keep people chained to the past.

2. Hope motivates. Hope helps you bounce back.

What is the difference between people who thrive and people who decline over a long period of time? It's not that they don't get knocked down; it's that they bounce back up. Every successful person I can think of has had to come back from discouraging circumstances. That's true of people I know personally and those I read about in the Bible. As a matter of fact, every single person in the Bible is a comeback story from *something*.

Check out this list and see if you can find yourself:

- Joseph endured mistreatment from a dysfunctional family. I bet there isn't anyone who doesn't have some relative the others try not to sit next to at Christmas dinner.
- David bounced back from several devastating failures: moral, leadership, career, and even worse. Have any past failures? A great comeback is possible!
- Elijah suffered personal criticism. I speak to over twelve thousand people every weekend and thousands more by radio. Usually, people each week write in or come up to say something encouraging. I remember very little of that. But I can tell you every critical comment. Why do we remember the things we ought to forget, and forget the things we ought to remember?
- Nehemiah was discouraged with harsh political, legal, and social circumstances at the highest levels. He had wall-to-wall problems— literally.
- John Mark was rejected by a high-ranking Christian leader. I know people for whom one negative comment from an authority figure—be it a teacher, a pastor, or a coach—has marked them for life.
- Peter was disappointed with his inability to withstand pressure and also disappointed with himself. Sound familiar? My number one source of discouragement is, unfortunately, myself.

- Jesus was let down by people of all types—friends, relatives, religious leaders. At His hour of greatest need, He takes three guys and says, "I need your support." When He comes back, they are fast asleep.

Every person in the Bible had to bounce back from something. (Lazarus even had to come back from being dead!) In almost every case, whether somebody bounces back or not has to do with one question: "Does that person have hope?" Hope looks at what can be instead of what is. Hope looks at the future rather than just the past. Hope believes in future possibility rather than resigning to current reality. People bounce back when they have *hope*.

3. Hope initiates. Hope sets you free to dream.

Nobody ever gets a dream without hope. I know of many leaders around the world, some blessed with great resources and others who have almost nothing, who have made major impacts on their communities. They all have the one thing nobody can do without—*hope*.

Hope gives birth to dreams, which creates momentum. I often tell leaders, "Momentum attracts support. It leads to personal renewal, relational renewal, and organizational renewal. Momentum and vision keep your ministry future-focused. But without hope, you won't have momentum. And without momentum, you're in trouble."

Hope sparks dreams, and dreams bring into existence some incredible initiatives. Every one of those initiatives started with hope. Corrie ten Boom hoped for freedom for Jews in the Netherlands. Martin Luther King had enough hope to have a dream of better days ahead for every person who had faced discrimination. Malala Yousafzai in Pakistan took a bullet to the head because she believes in better days ahead when girls can attend school. Dr. Carolyn Koons, a professor at Azusa Pacific University, launched the largest student mission in the world because she believed that God had better days ahead for every underresourced person in northern Mexico.

Last year, the high school kids in our church had a dream to build a child survival program in Dandora, Kenya. These kids raised fifty thousand dollars and sent it to Kenya. The year before, some students had heard about a homeless couple with three children living outside of Mexicali, Mexico. Their youngest child had died of exposure. Our students gave up their spring break, went down to Mexicali, and built this family a home. Other members of our church built more homes. But that one family is now in a safe place and their kids are out of the cold because a group of high school students had a dream that the world could be a better place for them. Those kinds of dreams don't happen without hope.

4. Hope activates. Hope is the fuel that makes the world a better place.

Like almost nothing else, hope has a way of unleashing compassion. This has proven true from the very start of the church.

Dr. D. James Kennedy pointed out that despite the church starting with a small band of discouraged disciples, it became the greatest force for good in all of history. Among its accomplishments, the church brought about hospitals, universities, literacy for the masses, capitalism, free enterprise, representative government, the separation of political powers, civil liberties, the abolition of slavery, modern science, discovery of the New World, the elevation of women, the Good Samaritan ethic of charity, high standards of justice, elevation of the common man, the value of human life, the work ethic, the codifying and writing of many of the world's languages, the preservation of human life through condemnation of perversions and elevation of healthy lifestyle practices, and a greater development and inspiration for music and art.[8]

Hope is the fuel that makes the world a better place. Hope helps people believe that they can make a difference, regardless of their circumstances.

This is something I see every time we visit Africa. Every November, I take teams of leaders to Nairobi, Kenya. I love the people. I love the culture. I love the grandeur and beauty, and I love seeing what people of hope can accomplish. Every year, we visit the same vibrant church in the slum of Dandora. The streets are dangerous, but the people are warmhearted.

Despite its poverty, this church has an AIDS center, runs a jobs program, and houses a school for three hundred children—all in facilities that are so inadequate you would never imagine that anything could happen. This place is transforming their community. Why is this place having such a positive effect? One dynamite woman with hope named Hilda.

In 2007, on my second visit, I walked into the church, and Hilda, whom I'd met the year before, greeted me with, "Hey, what are *you* doing here?"

"I was here a year ago," I said. "I fell in love with you guys. I just wanted to come back."

She paused, stared at me, and said, "*Nobody* comes back. Everybody says they'll come back, but they never do. *Nobody* comes back. Why are you *really* here?"

"I'm sorry," I said, "but you're stuck with me. We just want to have a friendship and see how we can serve your community together."

Hilda led me to a structure built to be a worship center. It had no windows, and the floor was mud. It had the potential to be a good building, but as it stood, it wasn't usable. The three hundred children under her care desperately needed to use this building. She took me on a tour.

"What do you use this for?" I asked.

"We can't use it," she said. "It's too muddy."

"What would it take to make it usable? You have three hundred kids with no place to meet."

"We've been saving money to put pebbles on the floor," she said. "At least that will soak up the water."

"When did you start this project?"

"Fifteen years ago," she said, "just as the economy went down."

"*Fifteen years?*"

"Yes," she said, "and it's going to happen! Once a week I come and take off my shoes because this is holy ground. I pray that God will do a miracle and we will finish this building and the children will be able to use it."

Then she looked me straight in the eye and said, "This is going to happen."

There is a lot of power in one person having hope. Back home, our church gathered leaders, raised money, and returned a year later. Scores of people from the community and fifteen guys from our church rebuilt the entire floor with concrete instead of just pebbles. That building has been used to reach that community ever since.

Our teams have now returned seven times. We all work side by side on various projects. On one trip, I knew a contested election had sparked riots across Kenya and angry mobs had torched practically everything since our last visit. Hilda greeted me, then said, "You have got to see this." She dragged me over to the fence.

"Look over there. What do you see?" Everything had been burned and blackened—except the church.

"Do you know what happened?" she said. "When the riots broke out, everybody hid in their houses. But when the mobs started to approach the church, the women of the community ran out of their houses and stood in front of the building. 'You will not torch this church,' they insisted. 'This is where our children get help.' The mobs walked right by the church, and it was left untouched."

I was standing in the middle of what looked like a war zone, listening to a lady who has very few resources but who has a huge heart and even greater hope. Her church building still stands today, instead of lying in a smoldering heap like the buildings around it. Why? Because her hope infected her neighborhood. Her unyielding compassion, fueled by hope, deeply encouraged her destitute community and, in turn, emboldened its members to seek ways to spread that compassion.

Adequate resources don't change the world. People with hearts strengthened by hope change the world!

Faith and Love . . . but Where's the Hope?

Anyone who has been to a Christian wedding has heard this famous Bible verse—1 Corinthians 13:13—"And now these three remain: faith, hope and love." Christians and Christianity will never thrive without all three. However, the Christian church has spent years majoring on two and leaving hope out of the equation.

We major in faith. Every church has a statement of faith. You can't get hired to work at a church without agreeing to one. You could fill stadiums with books on faith. I crammed three years of seminary into five years to study the Christian faith.

We major in love. We sing about it, talk about it, practice it, fill libraries with books about it, and nearly every movie has it as a theme. Faith and love get a lot of attention.

Few ever talk about hope. There are no classes on it. There are no Statements of Hope. God puts it in the list of the top three human essentials, yet for decades we have left it on the shelf.

God clearly values hope a great deal more than most of us who follow Him. I have eight years of advanced education and have sat through scores of classes and thousands of lectures, and amazingly, the subject of hope never came up. Not once!

While I have come to see hope as the most critical ingredient to success in life, family, and leadership, not one word was said about it. No wonder so many of God's people are faithful, caring, and yet deeply discouraged.

It is true:

- Hope liberates.
- Hope unleashes compassion.
- Hope encourages people.
- Hope motivates.
- Hope helps people attempt new things.
- Hope motivates people to find new strength.
- Hope propels people forward—even when it seems impossible.

What Hope Is Not

Hope is more than just an emotion you feel; it's a state of being you create.

Hope can be learned. Hope is the by-product of seven key factors that combine in a powerful way to make hope grow and thrive. We'll spend a lot of time focusing on those seven just a little later. In the next chapter, we'll see how hope is fed by encouragement and killed through discouragement.[9]

Hope is not some unreliable sensation.

Feelings are inconsistent. They come and go. Wishing is not hope. Positive thinking is not hope. Goal setting is not hope. Hope is something you intentionally build into your life. You do that by putting into practice seven hope-building factors.

Regardless of how much we build it, or how little we utilize it, hope remains constant, undiminished, and always available.[10]

Hope is a forward-facing confidence. Maybe you've been in some places or gone through some years where the best view is in the rearview mirror. But hope has no hindsight. We never hope backward. We always hope forward. Hope connects us to our future and determines that future. We cannot last even a second without hope (Romans 5:4–5). Without hope, we would not walk outside or take even one step into the unseen world ahead of us. Hope is the expectation of *good to come*.

Hope is not wishful thinking or blind optimism.

Hope is not shorthand for some sort of Pollyanna, close-your-eyes-and-pretend-that-everything-is-fine attitude. Think of the guy who fell off the top of a twenty-story building. Halfway down, someone yelled out the window, "How are you doing?" The guy falling said, "So far, so good."

When I speak of hope, it is not to make you think, *The universe is going to give good things to me.* "The universe" doesn't give anything to anybody. The kind of hope on which I've built my life is a confident expectation that God has better days ahead. I get this idea directly from the Bible and what God tells me there about hope.

Hope is not an unnecessary luxury.

Not only is it one of three essentials of life, but hope is also the one necessary ingredient to create consistent, compounding success.

Will It Float?

David Letterman's old late-night segment "Will It Float?" once inspired our staff to fill a huge water tank, place it at the front of an auditorium, and ask three thousand people to vote which of a series of items would float. We collected a bunch of unusual objects: a can of Spam, a five-pound bag of flour, an egg, a gallon of milk, a Shaq bobblehead doll. It was pretty funny.

After everyone voted, we threw in the objects, one by one, and then asked everyone to stare at the tank to see what would happen.

- Egg: floated.
- Spam: sank.
- Gallon of milk: floated.
- Shaq bobblehead doll: the body sank but the head floated.
- Five-pound bag of flour: fell apart and turned the whole tank white.

I turned to the audience after the results and said, "Nobody does very well in marriage, in relationships, at work, psychologically, or in life in general if they're not buoyant. Getting down is part of life. Staying down is what will kill you. If any Christian tells you he's never been discouraged, he's lying. All of us are going to get down.

"You're going to get down this year. It's just going to happen. You may be there right now. But if you stay down, your education doesn't matter. Your theology doesn't matter. Your skill level doesn't matter. Your financial backing doesn't matter. If you get down and stay down, you will drown."

The only thing that will keep you from going under is hope. Hope makes you buoyant. Hope liberates. Hope motivates. Hope initiates. Hope activates. That's why hope is so important.

The polar opposite of hope is discouragement. It acts like a lead weight around your neck. When you feel discouraged, you lose buoyancy and sink. Nothing good comes from sinking, as we'll see in the next chapter.

3.

DISCOURAGEMENT
DESTROYS EVERYTHING

The LORD your God is bringing you into a good land, a land of brooks of water, of fountains and springs, that flow out of valleys.

DEUTERONOMY 8:7 NKJV

You don't drown by falling in the water. You drown by staying there.

EDWIN LOUIS COLE

A friend's vibrant seventy-year-old grandmother came home from the hospital after hip surgery. Accustomed to living alone, she was hobbling toward the kitchen to make lunch when she remembered her glasses on the nightstand. As she swiveled in the doorway to go back, her foot, raised due to being on crutches, hit the doorframe. Her daughter drove her back to the hospital, where doctors set her broken ankle. Late that afternoon she got back home and remembered trash collection was the next day. She took a small sack of trash, along with her house key, to the big metal barrel out front. Balancing on one crutch, she flung the bag into the barrel, but the key followed. She was quite short and the barrel was oversize, but she could see the key, so she reached in to fish it out. She got stuck. A neighbor saw her hanging on the side of the barrel and helped her, then drove her back to the hospital because her side hurt. The hospital treated her for a cracked rib then kept her overnight "for observation," which apparently was code for "don't let her break anything else." At her funeral twenty-six years later, her family smiled about the day her resourceful independence almost got the better of her.

Young or old, sick or healthy, all of us have days that feel just like that. The problem comes when those days result in discouragement, because discouragement is *deadly*.

A huge life principle I have learned the hard way is that *discouragement precedes destruction*. I cannot find anything that has been destroyed without discouragement being the underlying cause.

No person has ever come up to me and said, "I'm so encouraged about my marriage, I'm getting a divorce." No one has ever come up to me and said, "I am so encouraged about school, I'm dropping out." I have never had anybody come up to me and say, "I'm so encouraged about the church I'm attending, I'm leaving it." No teenager has ever come up to me and said, "I'm so encouraged about what my faith means to me, I'm going to start drinking and taking drugs." Ask any psychologist, ask any pastor, or ask any parent.

When discouragement is present, storm clouds are on the horizon. Something is going to be attacked and potentially destroyed. Every marriage that has broken up, every person who has given up, every company that has gone belly-up, every venture that has failed, every church that I have seen decline, every country that has gone downhill, and certainly every suicide ever committed, all shared one emotion—discouragement.

Discouragement devastates, and absolute discouragement devastates absolutely. In the absence of hope, discouragement rules. You won't find a more ruthless, negative, destructive, vicious dictator anywhere on the planet.

The Disease of Discouragement

Unchecked discouragement is not only a vicious dictator, but it's also a lethal disease. My friend Rick Warren says the "disease of discouragement" has four key characteristics. It is universal, repeating, deadly, and contagious, to which I'll add that it's also always circumstantial.[1]

1. *Discouragement is a universal disease. We all get it.*

It's true—everybody catches this disease at one time or another. No doctor has invented a vaccine that can prevent discouragement from entering your system. Discouragement *happens*. It's a fact of life. I'll prove it by asking you to answer just one question:

Have you felt discouraged at any time in the past two months?

If you said no, then you need some intensive coursework on lying. *All* of us get discouraged occasionally, even those of us blessed with normally upbeat natures. I am naturally upbeat. When I get discouraged, it usually doesn't last long. Have you ever taken a beach ball to the bottom of a pool and then let it go? God has wired me something like that. I know I can't afford to stay down, so I have learned what I need to do to help me get back up.

But even those who don't often get low still at times come down with the disease. Discouragement is universal.

A year before we started Bayside, the church I pastor in Sacramento, I got very low and stayed down for a long time. Carol and I had recently moved from Chicago, where I had been working as a seminary professor, and relocated to Folsom, California. Sometime after our move, a church where I had once served called me.

"Ray," the board member said, "we need a senior pastor. Are you interested?"

I didn't know if I was, but I felt flattered that they even called. At the time, I was traveling, writing, speaking, and having a great time *not* being a pastor. So I told him, "I'm not sure it's the right thing, but let me pray about it."

"Great," he said, "let's both pray about it. Send us your résumé."

I sent them my résumé and then heard nothing for nearly four months. Eventually I received a letter from the church, but it sounded nothing like the personal call from months before. Have you ever received one of those "Dear Occupant in Christ" form letters? That's what it felt like. It might as well have said, "Dear wannabe pastor who wrote us, thank you for applying for the position of senior pastor of our church." Well, number one, I *hadn't* applied. *They* had contacted *me*. Then it said, in essence, "Unfortunately, we don't feel as though you're even close to being the right person, so take a hike." I'm sure they phrased the bad news more tactfully, but that's what it felt like. As I sat there reading this dismissive letter, I felt totally rejected.

It felt very much like a little girl approaching a boy and asking, "Would you like to ask me out?"

"Well, I guess so," replies the boy.

"Oh, so you'd like to go out?" the girl says. "No thanks."

That experience of rejection hurt my feelings and sent me into an emotional tailspin. I stayed in that dark place of discouragement longer than usual. I thought, *God, what are You up to? Why is this happening to me?*

I had no idea that God was up to something *way* beyond anything I could imagine. Even in my deep hurt and discouragement, He was working out a far better plan. For the last eighteen years, I have watched God work in the church we started the year *after* that experience. It has blown away anything I ever dreamed. But I knew nothing of it at that moment, and I wouldn't for months. I could only see rejection and feel the discouragement.

Discouragement happens. To everyone. Including me.

2. Discouragement is a repeating disease. You will catch it more than once.

I wish discouragement was like chicken pox—get it once, done, it's over. Discouragement is not like that. Discouragement is a disease that repeats as often as you let it.

I was leaving my house yesterday morning to start this chapter. On the way out, Carol asked, "How are you doing?"

I said, "I'm a little bit discouraged."

"Where are you going?"

"I'm going to write a chapter on discouragement."

Welcome to real life. Discouragement is a repeating disease; you'll catch it as often as you allow it to come in.

3. Discouragement is a contagious disease. You can catch it from discouraging people.

Most of us would never dream about spending a lot of time in a confined space with somebody who has a contagious disease. Discouragement is even deadlier than some contagious diseases. In fact, it's often easier to recover from sickness than from the disease of discouragement.

People can easily catch the virus of discouragement from the discouraging people around them. When I spend fifteen minutes with an energy-sapping person, I walk out discouraged, no matter how I walked in.

You could boil down the whole human race to two types of people: those who build people up and those who tear people down. When you spend time with someone who majors in tearing you down, discouragement becomes extremely contagious.

If you and I were able to sit down for a cup of coffee, and I were to ask who the discouraging people in your life are, I'll bet names would come immediately to your mind. It could be a friend, it could be a boss, it could be a neighbor, it could be an in-law (you may even have outlaws instead of in-laws). You know that when you are going to be around these people, discouragement comes with the territory.

A few years ago, my wife and I made a decision that if someone was too discouraging, we wouldn't spend much social time with that person. What I realized is this—the father I'm called to be, the husband I'm called to be, the pastor I'm called to be, and the Christian I'm called to be and what I'm called to do are just too important, and I need to be at my best. There is no way I can be at my best in any of those areas if I am discouraged.

So I watch who I hang out with. And honestly, I would fly across the country to spend the day with somebody who is encouraging.

4. Discouragement is always circumstantial. It always has a cause.

The following story appeared in an editorial column in the *New York Times Magazine* and has been told with many variations.

A crew was plucked out of the Sea of Japan, dazed and clinging to the wreckage of their sunken ship. Authorities jailed them after asking, "What caused your ship to sink?" To a man, each sailor claimed that a cow, falling out of the clear, blue sky, landed on their ship, smashed through the deck, and sank the vessel. No doubt the disbelieving officials thought, *Okay, where's the sake? Get out the Breathalyzer!* They immediately threw the men in prison, certain they had to be lying. I mean, a *cow*?

The sailors remained behind bars for several weeks, deeply discouraged, until the Russian Air Force called. The Russians prefaced their remarks with, "We're not going to take any responsibility for this." They then informed Japanese authorities that the crew of one of their large cargo planes had apparently stolen a cow that had been wandering around the edge of a Siberian airfield. The airmen had loaded the cow into the hold and hastily taken off, planning to take the animal home. No one had rigged the plane to carry live cargo, so while in flight, the frightened cow rampaged back and forth in the cargo hold. The flyers feared that the raging beast would cause the plane to crash, so to save the cargo, the aircraft, and themselves, they opened the cargo door and shoved the cow out at thirty thousand feet over the Sea of Japan. The boat never saw it coming.

The story has been debunked as an urban legend, but it really did make the *New York Times Magazine*, and it's a great story, even if it's fiction.[2]

Sometimes, discouraging circumstances seem to drop out of nowhere. Most of the discouraging circumstances that have hit my life, I never saw coming. All discouragement that has parachuted into my life has come from one of three sources:

 1. *Circumstances.* Stuff happens: unexpected bills, health problems, taxes go up again.

 2. *Other people.* Somebody says something negative or does something hurtful.

 3. *Me.* My main source of discouragement is myself.

Anyone can get hit with circumstances that trigger discouragement—even if you happen to be one of the most famous prophets of all time. In the familiar Old Testament story, what four hundred prophets of Baal couldn't do, one woman was able to accomplish. Jezebel, outraged that Elijah's God trumped her false prophets, screamed an oath that she would kill him (1 Kings 19).

I once did a study on this Bible story and wrote a sermon titled "When People Lose Hope." What Elijah did when he lost hope, we also do when we lose hope. Elijah, deeply discouraged, made things worse by doing five things in rapid succession, all of them destructive:

1. He started making rash, unhealthy decisions.
2. He ran from responsibility.
3. He blamed other people.
4. He completely lost perspective.
5. He gave up too soon.

Sound familiar? All five of these responses resonate with me. I also wish that Elijah and I were exceptions to the rule, but I know we're not.

How do you deal with discouragement? Chances are mighty slim that a cow will drop out of the sky anytime soon (although you might want to look up every now and then). But chances are very good that the other circumstances, perhaps just as random, will drop in to shatter the calm of your life.

5. Discouragement is deadly. It kills.

Discouragement can wreck lives, ruin relationships, and destroy dreams. I've watched discouragement shatter a person's career. I've watched discouragement demolish a person's relationship with God. I've watched discouragement incinerate a family. I've seen discouragement destroy entire churches when the spirit of the congregation became the spirit of discouragement.

John Toole was a young man who wrote a book shortly after he got out of the army. Since John thought his work had some promise, he shopped it around to various publishers, getting nothing but rejection after rejection. He kept going, however, because he had a dream to become a writer.

The continual rejections eventually took their toll, however, and finally John gave up. But his mom never did. She just kept shopping the book around. She went from publisher to publisher, having no better luck than her son, until one day she read that an author was becoming a professor at Loyola University New Orleans. "My son wrote a book based in New Orleans," she told him when she pushed her way into his office. "Maybe, since you're a writer, you'd like it." He agreed to read the manuscript, and he loved it. He soon sold it to Louisiana State University Press.

Nobody knew that the manuscript would turn into a best seller on ten different lists. And in 1981, John Toole's book *A Confederacy of Dunces* won the Pulitzer Prize for fiction. Unfortunately, he couldn't accept the award. His mother accepted it for him, but not for any happy reason. You see, when John Toole gave up on his dream in 1969, he gave up on more than his dream. Stung by multiple rejections, he took his life, just a dozen years before his literary work would surpass his wildest imagination.[3]

Discouragement precedes destruction. Discouragement is a killer. When it comes rapping at your door, how will you keep it at bay?

Discouragement is universal, repeating, contagious, and ultimately deadly. It will wreck your life, and it will wreck your relationships. You *will* get down—the key is not to stay there!

How can you get back up? With seven factors that act as antidotes to discouragement. The seven are so powerful, you'll want to keep reading.

PART TWO

SEVEN FACTORS THAT RAISE YOUR HOPE QUOTIENT

⚠ WARNING

THE FOLLOWING INFORMATION IS KNOWN TO RAISE LEVELS OF HOPE, PRODUCE FRESH VISION, AND INCREASE ENERGY

4.

THE SEVEN

You will harvest what you plant.

Galatians 6:7 cev

Great things are not done by impulse, but by a series of small things brought together.

Vincent van Gogh

On November 9, 1965, at 5:16 p.m., events were set into motion that brought one of the richest, most industrialized, and highly populated areas of the Western world to a complete standstill. A backup relay switch at the Sir Adam Beck power station in Ontario, Canada, was accidentally set too low to handle increasing power transmissions, and it tripped. The power cascaded to the next line, which overloaded and transferred to the next, shutting them down one after another. In less than five minutes, the entire Northeast power grid went offline.

The results were unimaginable. New York City was blacked out within ten minutes.

There was no power to provide heat or light to citizens or to allow them to communicate. There was no power to operate pumps, move sewage, or deliver water and gas. The power needed to run life-support systems at hospitals was cut off. During the evening rush hour, an estimated eight hundred thousand people were trapped in subways. Only half of one hundred fifty hospitals had emergency power available. At the JFK airport, two hundred fifty flights had to be diverted.

With no light, no heat, and no communications, thirty million people found themselves in a dark, silent, frightening new world. All because of a ripple effect set in motion by a small switch in a metal cup—a relay that was set too low.[1]

This book is intended to start a ripple effect in *you*. Small things can make a dramatic difference in your life. Becoming a person with hope—defeating discouragement and building a new future—is *always* a result of raising seven hope factors, which I call The Seven.

Anything Is Possible

Building The Seven into your life will increase your hope level dramatically. Raising these seven will free you and fuel you to catch a fresh vision for your future. And when that happens, *anything is possible.*

Recently, I spoke about The Seven at a weeklong conference. When the chart lit up the screen, I could hear people throughout the crowd say, "Got it!" I told them, as I'm telling you now, "I'm not talking so much about hope but about seven critical factors that, when they are rising in your life, will give you genuine hope."

Let me tell you how important this is to me. Every year, I set goals. Sometimes they go well; sometimes they don't. Five years ago, I had one goal for the whole year. I was going to work for 365 days to do one thing—raise my hope level. My goal was to be more hope-filled at the end of the year than I was at the start of the year.

By that time, I had learned that hope would improve my relationships, my marriage, and my impact, and I would be a whole lot more fun to be around. Not too long into that year, though, I realized I couldn't raise my hope level by wishing to be more hopeful.

You raise your hope level by investing in The Seven. The ripple effect will be life changing. Let me show you exactly what this looks like.

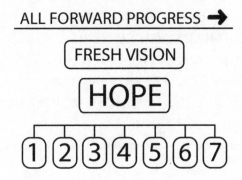

Now, let me walk you through this from the top. Here goes:

- All forward progress (anything great that ever happens in your life and future) comes from fresh vision.
- All fresh vision comes from hope (discouraged people don't dream).
- And hope thrives when you focus on elevating these seven essential life practices, or hope factors.

Here are The Seven:

1. *Recharge your batteries.* Nobody does well running on empty.
2. *Raise your expectations.* You don't get what you deserve; you get what you expect.
3. *Refocus on the future.* It's time to throw away your rearview mirror. No one goes forward well when they are looking back.
4. *Play to your strengths.* Be yourself; everyone else is taken.
5. *Refuse to go it alone.* Never underestimate the power of support. Even the Lone Ranger had Tonto.
6. *Replace burnout with balance.* Burning the candle at both ends isn't as bright as you think.
7. *Play great defense.* Avoid these five toxic hope killers that can threaten your future.

These Seven change everything! Why? Because . . .
RAISING THESE **SEVEN** FACTORS
RAISES YOUR **HOPE** QUOTIENT . . .
which CREATES **FRESH VISION**
which UNLEASHES A WHOLE **NEW FUTURE**!

If you want a new, better, and more fulfilling future—build these seven hope factors.

If you want less discouragement, anxiety, and fear—build these seven hope factors.

If you want more confidence and healthier emotions—build these seven hope factors.

If you want to bring out the best in your kids—build these seven hope factors.

If you want to raise positive teenagers—build these seven hope factors.

If you want to break bad habits—build these seven hope factors.

If you want to change the environment at work—build these seven hope factors.

Why is raising your Hope Quotient job one? Simple—the ripple effect. Raising these seven leads to hope, which leads to fresh vision, which leads to great new things in your life, health, finances, and future. In short, raising your HQ changes everything, because you will finally be living with a *solid, secure, emotionally healthy, and spiritually solid foundation.*

Hope Needs a Solid Foundation

The Chase Manhattan Bank building, coincidentally located in Manhattan, is a sixty-story, massive skyscraper. When it was being built, halfway through the construction, they discovered what no builder ever wants to learn—the monster structure was not being built on rock as the engineers had thought but was being built on *quicksand.* At some point soon, if they didn't fix it, the building would sink, topple over, and destroy part of Manhattan. Something had to be done.

Engineers explored the possibilities of dismantling the framework or somehow shoring it up with caissons or pilings. Geologists were brought in who advised that it would take, oh, about a million years for the quicksand to solidify. Then someone came up with an innovative idea. They sank pipes deep into the quicksand and forced a solution of sodium silicate and calcium chloride into it. In just a few days, the quicksand turned into solid, watertight sandstone, and they were able to finish the building. Injecting the additives was ingenious.[2]

The Seven that I'm about to list for you make up factors that, when built into your marriage, career, parenting, and all areas of life, will strengthen you and create a solid foundation. The Seven are so important that we spent the last year developing an online assessment you can take to identify where you are now and what you need. The next seven chapters are designed to help you inject these into your life.

Now that you know why I believe the most important thing anybody can do is stay encouraged and raise their HQ, it's time to begin the process of measuring—and raising—your Hope Quotient. Included with this book is a unique code that will allow you to take the assessment and receive a customized action plan based on the results.

Here's how to get started:

1. Find your unique access code on the nonprinted side of the cover. It will be covered with foil that you will have to scratch off, revealing the code. *Please note that your book will NOT be returnable once the foil has been scratched off.*
2. Go to HopeQuotient.com and enter your code in the box in the upper right-hand corner.
3. Complete the registration process.
4. Once the registration process is complete, you will be taken to the HQ assessment. Remember, the code allows one person to take the test one time, so be sure to take the test when you have the time and concentration necessary to take it from start to finish. The test itself takes less than ten minutes on average.

5. Entering the code and completing the registration process will not only allow you to take the assessment, but it will also serve as the key to unlock your personal HQ level.

6. If you encounter any issues, you can e-mail us at support@ HopeQuotient.com. We're here to help.

Once you've taken the test, buckle up—you're going to love this ride.

5.

ONE: RECHARGE YOUR BATTERIES

They shall mount up with wings as eagles; they shall run, and not be weary; and they shall walk, and not faint.

ISAIAH 40:31 KJV

Untended fires soon become nothing more than a pile of ashes.

GAIL McDONALD

I live near Beale Air Force Base, one of the few pilot training grounds for the famous U-2 spy planes. Some U-2 pilots attending our church have given me a real education. Sitting in a "chase car" going a hundred miles an hour, fifty feet away from a massive U-2 with a wingspan of 103 feet, watching a masterful pilot deftly balance the "Dragon Lady" on one wheel to coast to a slow stop . . . you can't help but think, *No question. These are the best pilots in the world.*

Quite possibly the most famous U-2 pilot of all time was Francis Gary Powers. On May 1, 1960, Powers took off from a military base in Peshawar, Pakistan, to fly a reconnaissance mission seventy thousand feet above the Soviet Union. But earlier that spring, the Soviets had developed a surface-to-air missile that could reach the high-flying U-2s, and they shot down Powers's plane. Powers ejected from his crippled craft and was captured, convicted of espionage, and sentenced to three years in prison and seven years of hard labor. Instead, he was released in two years, when the United States agreed to a prisoner swap for a KGB master spy. After his release, he went on to pilot a series of the world's most dangerous experimental aircraft. Powers worked as a Lockheed test pilot and finally became a helicopter traffic reporter. What a survivor.

Years later, Powers lost his life in another crash. He was piloting a standard traffic helicopter for an LA television station when it went down. Why did he crash? Simple. His helicopter ran out of gas.[1]

Unbelievable!

After surviving a U-2 crash, Soviet prison, and thousands of experimental flights, he went down . . . *because he ran out of gas.*

Running on empty is a really bad life strategy.

You Need Your Engine *On*

I learned firsthand about flying without power. A friend of mine is a professor of aeronautical engineering at the University of California at Davis. He called one day and invited me to lunch. When I got to his office, we hopped in his car, but instead of going to a restaurant, he drove to the private UC Davis airport and pulled out a brown paper sack.

"Here's lunch," he said. "I thought we could eat and talk while we fly." I looked at the single-engine prop plane in front of us and thought, *Isn't there a Denny's nearby?*

We took off and had climbed to about six thousand feet when he looked over and said, "Would you like to see what it's like to weigh twice what you weigh now?" (Have you ever aspired to weigh *twice* your weight?) Before I could answer, he took the plane straight up in the air. My stomach, along with the sandwich I just swallowed, dropped into my shoes.

He leveled off, and I thought we were done with the stunt maneuvers. Then he said, "Would you like to see what it would be like to be weightless?" Before I could say no, he pointed the nose straight down. Everything started floating in the cockpit, and my sandwich was now lodged in my brain. He finally leveled off again, and I thought, *I'm so glad that's over. You're insane!*

Then he said, "Would you like to see what it's like to be six thousand feet up with no running engine?"

By this time I was unable to speak, but he wasn't looking for answers anyway, because by the time he said the word *engine*, he had reached up and turned the engine switch *off*! The amazing thing was, *nothing* happened! It made no difference. The plane didn't dive. We kept right on going. I thought, *This is interesting. You can be six thousand feet in the air in a single-engine plane with no running engine, and you're fine.* Then I thought, *But only for a while, because if that engine doesn't restart . . .*

Just as I was picturing the crash and imagining my wife at the funeral wondering where I even met this guy, my friend regained his sanity, started the engine, and headed home. We landed safely, and I have never accepted a lunch invitation from him again. But I did introduce him to Carol, just in case.

I learned in a dramatic way that everything that flies, everything that goes forward, everything that stays up, stays up because it's *fueled* and the engine is *on*.

What Fuels You?

If everything that moves in this world runs on fuel, what is it that fuels you?

You can be the most gifted and experienced person in the world, but when you run out of fuel, you're going to crash and burn. Refueling is one of the most important things in life. Your skill level, your talent, your educational background—everything can be going for you, but if you end up on empty, you're due for a fall. Across thirty-five years of working with people, the number one thing people need to hear from me is—*make sure your batteries are recharged!*

- I recently met with a business executive whose company is fighting to stay afloat. He asked if I had any advice. I said, "Absolutely! Keep your emotional and spiritual batteries recharged and you will have all the strength you need to face challenging times."

- I met a young mom with two kids whose life was turned upside down a few weeks ago when her husband walked out on her. I said, "You may not control what your husband does, but you do have control over one thing. Keep your spiritual batteries recharged and you'll be in better shape to get your kids and yourself through this."
- Two weeks ago, a high school senior told me his friends had been trying to drag him away from his faith and values. Sharp kid. Sharp enough to know he didn't want to go that direction. I said, "You have no control over how your friends treat you, but you have absolute control over whether your spiritual batteries are charged. If they are, you'll have strength even when your friends try to take you down a road you don't want to go."
- Last week I met with a young pastor in his first ministry position. It only took him a few months to realize that seminary didn't prepare him for the complex leadership, management, and relational challenges he faced. I said, "Your single most important leadership step is to learn to stay encouraged—and that only happens if you keep your spiritual, emotional, and relational batteries charged."

Those are just four examples of recent conversations. I realize over and over again, from pastors to teens, from moms to managers, from employers to employees, to all people trying to build a future: *the road to a better future is never traveled on an empty tank.*

Why? Because drained people are more susceptible to the toxic emotions of fear, anxiety, and discouragement. Drained people make bad decisions. Drained people do not respond well, feel well, or live well.

Every person needs to ask these questions:

What drains me?
and
What fuels me?

And that's why the number one principle for increasing your HQ is:

Recharge your batteries!

Pay Attention to What's Draining You

If it's true that the most important thing for a person to do is stay encouraged (and it is!), then every person has to answer the questions, *What discourages me?* and *What drains me?* This is called playing good defense. It's so important that we have an entire chapter on it later. For now, let me give the reason it's important.

A couple of years ago, I went through a season when I was more tired, discouraged, and touchy (and my wife would probably say more *grouchy*) than usual. A friend suggested I take a ten-year look back at my life in leadership and track high points and low points. It worked! Charting the highs and lows helped me see that almost every season of my life when I was thriving, productive, and helpful to the most amount of people was a season when I was encouraged and at my best. Almost every season when I was not thriving came right after a season when I was running on empty.

As a pastor and a parent, I realized I would have to make sure not to allow too many things in my life that could discourage or deplete me. Your future is too important, and your family matters too much to allow yourself to be drained by the things that sap your energy. The trick is, this is different for everyone. What drains me may not drain you. Simply knowing what drains you can help you develop a plan to refuel.

I'll give you one small example. Carol and I have four kids. When our twins were born, we had four kids under five years old. A buddy of mine said that having little children is like having a bowling alley installed in your mind. We had multiple lanes going at all times. When Carol once left for a week, and I had the kids alone, I understood better that though children are gifts from the Lord they can be some of the most exhausting gifts in the world.

I realized that for a full-time parent, there were going to be days that were just too draining. I was working on a college campus, so Carol and I offered our spare bedroom to some college students to live in. In exchange, they helped prepare dinner and were available from one to five to watch the kids if Carol wanted to leave the house. This was awesome. My marriage got better. My wife's encouragement level got better. I got happier. Our kids were happier. Everybody was happier simply by paying attention to something that had the potential to be both joyful and draining, and developing a plan to refuel.

There are some things so draining that you just need to get rid of them. Motivational speaker Gail Blanke wrote a great book a few years ago, *Throw Out Fifty Things*. The message was to eliminate the clutter, physical *or* emotional, that holds you back.[2]

Five Passion Killers

To increase your Hope Quotient, take stock and see what nonessential things are draining you; then get rid of them. For most people, myself included, some things are far too draining to keep in your life. Let me give you a list of five of them. These five passion killers will exhaust your fuel supply and cause you to crash and burn.

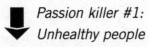

Passion killer #1:
Unhealthy people

Emotionally unhealthy people are draining people. We all have them in our lives. How can you tell who they are? They're the people you have to recover from after you're around them. When you see some people coming, you think, *Oh, great!* When you see other people coming, you wince, *Oh, no!*

Carol and I have both kinds of people in our lives, the people who build us up and the people who tear us down. As I mentioned in chapter 3, some people are so negative that, although we love them, we don't spend much time with them. We cannot afford to become the type of people we might become by spending too much time with them. You might think, *Can I be around only perfect people?* Absolutely not! I am saying that to have a high HQ and get your batteries recharged, your *primary* relationships have to be with people who build you up.

Passion killer #2:
Unkind critics

It's important to listen to advice and feedback, but remember, the world is full of unkind critics who don't have your destiny in mind. We all have people in our lives who think they have a "spiritual gift" of criticism and want to "help" the Holy Spirit. It helped me when I heard a speaker use an old expression this way: "Listening to your critics is like bobbing for apples in a vat of acid." Listening to your critics will drain your passion. Avoid unkind critics to keep spiritually charged.

Passion killer #3:
Unbalanced schedule

An unbalanced schedule is so draining that we will tackle it in detail in a later chapter. A friend of mine says, "If you're burning the candle at both ends, you're not as bright as you think you are." If you're about to burn out right now, just put your finger here and flip over to chapter 10 *fast*. I'll be here waiting for you when you finish.

Passion killer #4:
Unnecessary guilt

You cannot feel enthusiasm and guilt at the same time. Unconfessed sin and the unnecessary guilt that results from it will kill your passion. This point is not written to make you feel guiltier. Most of us are already guilt sponges. The message of the Bible, the central reason Jesus went to the cross, is that God wants to forgive you *for* your past and also free you *from* your past. The least healthy thing a human ever does is get stuck in the past and look backward with regret. The apostle Paul said, "Forgetting the past and looking forward to what lies ahead" (Philippians 3:13 NLT). Few things steal our joy more quickly and rob our passion faster than being saturated by guilt. Guilt will lock you in a self-imposed prison of regret.

There is a better way. My friend Lee Strobel said, "What kind of God is this, who prefers the human reclamation business to the human condemnation business? . . . When you get an accurate picture of who He is, He's awfully hard to resist."[3]

 Passion killer #5:
Underestimating the impact of exposure

What we think about determines who we will become. Two friends, John Maxwell and John Ortberg, teach on this topic, and I borrowed from both of them. Let's just say I'm quoting from First John and Second John.

First, *your mind will think most about whatever you most expose it to.* This is the impact of exposure. What enters your mind repeatedly will be revealed in your character and life.

Nobody in NASCAR fills a high-performance car with low-octane gas. Nobody trying out for the Olympics goes on a Twinkies-and-chocolate diet. When people have kids, they are pretty careful about what goes into that child (or at least the *first* child!). As a general rule, we're careful about what we put into something valuable, because we know that what we put into it determines its performance and well-being. So it astounds me that people disregard the impact of exposure in the most important area of life—our minds.

Second, the law of exposure says that the events you attend, the materials you read, the music you hear, the images you watch, and the daydreams you engage in are shaping your mind and ultimately shaping your actions, character, and destiny. The law of exposure is as predictable as the law of gravity. The law of gravity doesn't surprise anybody. Nobody steps off a ledge, falls ten feet, and says, "What were the odds of that happening?" But people violate the law of exposure all the time and act with total shock when what they expose themselves to profoundly shapes their lives.

Develop Your Supply Lines

These five passion killers will drain you and leave you empty. Avoiding them is the first part of keeping yourself fully energized—but not the only part. Progress stops when the supply line of fuel gets cut. Military buffs know that one of the biggest factors in any war is always the supply line logistics to fuel the troops.

Near the start of World War II, German Field Marshall Erwin Rommel practically drove the British out of Northern Africa, earning the respect of both friend and foe, and the nickname "Desert Fox." But by the fall of 1941, Rommel found himself forced to retreat almost to his original position. Why? One factor turned victory to defeat—he ran ahead of his supply lines. Rommel's army basically ran out of gas.[4]

Staying encouraged requires developing five supply lines that will keep you spiritually and emotionally fueled.

 Supply line #1:
Invest in your own growth.

As a young man, I was privileged to have lunch one day with a man I greatly admired. After listening to my life plans for a while, he looked across the table and said, "I have one question. The most important thing to your impact, leadership, and ministry is—*you*. I want to know, what are you doing, year by year, to invest in your own growth and development?"

The question had never occurred to me. I doubt it occurs to a lot of us. Most parents think about their child's growth. Executives think about their company's growth. Teachers think about their students' growth. Most human beings reach a point where they have invested in everybody's growth but have never sat down to think about investing in their own.

Allow me to ask you the question he asked. *What are you doing, year by year, to invest in your own growth and development?*

Even Jesus Christ, the perfect Son of the living God, took time to recharge His batteries. The Gospels are packed with "Jesus withdrew . . ." and "Jesus "prayed . . ." To say, "I don't have time!" is another way of saying, "I prefer to be drained and hopeless." I can't tell you the best way to withdraw and recharge. That varies from person to person. But I do know that even the busiest people—if they are men and women full of hope—find a way that works for them.

Seven years ago, we launched Thrive, an annual leadership conference. We had one goal: pack a conference with so much octane and so many options that anyone wanting inspiration and growth would never recover. Without marketing, it sold out three months in advance last year, with four thousand people from thirty states and six countries. My favorite moment last year was when a well-known leader came up to me at the end and said, "Thank you! I come every year and I'll tell you why. This is where I meet God. This is where I let go of the past year. This is where I catch fresh vision. This is where I get equipped to live and lead in the next year." A brilliant compliment from a brilliant leader, one smart enough to invest in his own growth.

 Supply line #2:
Understand the power of worship.

The minute they hear the word *worship*, some people respond like the boy who asked the Sunday school teacher, "Can't we hurry? This is *boring*!" The little girl next to him said, "Shh! This is supposed to be boring. It's church."

The Bible says the exact opposite. Isaiah wrote that those who wait on the Lord will renew their strength (Isaiah 40:31). That's not all it does:

- Authentic worship renews your strength.
- Authentic worship reconnects you with God.
- Authentic worship restores your perspective.
- Authentic worship rekindles your hope.
- Authentic worship rebuilds your confidence.
- Authentic worship restores your joy.
- Authentic worship releases your anxieties.

Worship is so powerful that every seven days, God says, "Here's a prescription: take a day off and do this."

Worship refocuses me on God. When I think about my agenda and how little or how poorly I'm doing or being treated or not accomplishing, it's crushing. As it turns out, thinking about me too much is not even healthy. Famed psychologist Martin Seligman blames skyrocketing rates of depression on "rampant individualism," the focus on self.[5] Worship gets my attention off myself.

The early days of aviation were full of firsts. Right before World War I, a man attempted to fly around the globe. He made it to the East Coast, landed in a pasture, fueled his plane, and took off for a four-hour flight over water to the next place he could safely land. Two hours later, he heard a scratching, gnawing sound inside the plane. The pilot realized that while he was on the ground, a rat had crawled in and was now gnawing on the steering cable. If it snapped, he'd plummet to his death into the ocean. With no way to fly quickly two hours forward or two hours back, he was filled with terror. Then he had a life-saving thought. Rats are made to live on the ground, not in the sky. He pulled the nose up and climbed up, up, up another two thousand feet. The gnawing stopped. He leveled his altitude, calmly flew on, landed, and threw out the dead rat.[6]

This is exactly what worship does. The rodents of your life aren't meant to live in the presence of God. Worship takes you to heights where worry, anxiety, stress, and fear wither away and cease to gnaw at your life. Why would you want to live any other way?

 Supply line #3:
Unleash the Bible into your life.

A few years ago, a Midwest church conducted a four-year nationwide study to investigate what factors most effectively cause spiritual growth and life transformation. After interviewing thousands of people from hundreds of churches, the "Reveal" study concluded, "The Bible is the most powerful catalyst for spiritual growth. *The Bible's power to advance spiritual growth is unrivaled by anything else.* Reflection on Scripture is by far the most influential spiritual practice."[7]

John Maxwell says that life transformation takes five steps:

1. When you change your *thinking*, you change your *beliefs*.
2. When you change your *beliefs*, you change your *expectations*.
3. When you change your *expectations*, you change your *attitude*.
4. When you change your *attitude*, you change your *behavior*.
5. When you change your *behavior*, you change your *life*![8]

The big idea is—*All great life change starts when I change the way I think.*

In his classic book *Spiritual Depression*, D. Martin Lloyd-Jones declares that too often we are listening to ourselves when we should be talking to ourselves. We should be preaching the Word of God to ourselves.[9]

If you lack inner strength, you will also lack hope. Hope never pours out of the lives of empty, depleted people. You get inner strength by unleashing the Bible into your life.

Imagine that I show you two cans of Coke. On the outside, they look just alike. "I bought them at the same place, same time," I tell you. When I squeeze one, I instantly crush it. Call me Superman! But when I squeeze the other, nothing happens. I mean, *nothing*. I can stand there and squeeze that can until my veins pop and my face goes red, but I can't even dent it, let alone crush it. My great strength has zero impact. What makes the difference?

You guessed it. The first can is empty. The second can is full.

Here's the principle: *inner strength is essential when you're under pressure.*

Inner strength can outlast anything. Nationwide surveys and my own experience say the same thing—if you want inner strength and life transformation, unleash the Bible into your life.

 Supply line #4:
Build great relationships.

What all of us have are people on our backs. What all of us need are people on our side. If you think this topic is unimportant, consider this:

- In his book *A Cry Unheard: New Insights into the Medical Consequences of Loneliness*, Dr. James Lynch cites a wealth of studies proving lonely people live significantly shorter lives.[10]

- University of Michigan researchers discovered lack of friendship is a health risk as high as obesity, smoking, and high blood pressure.[11]
- Dr. John Gottman, from the University of Washington, studied six hundred couples and concluded that friendship is the key to marital happiness.[12]
- Carnegie Institute studies reveal that 85 percent of financial success is due to skill with people.[13]
- The Bible is filled with friendships, such as David and Jonathan, Jesus and His disciples, Paul and Barnabas, and Mary and Elizabeth.

Psychologists tell us that American males struggle to have *any* close friendships.[14] Not long ago, I read about a former CEO who had led more than a million employees. When he went into the hospital to have a lung removed, he did not receive one card, one phone call, or one visit from any of those people.

In our culture, loneliness is rampant. We need good friends *especially* when we feel depleted. Friends can give us hope and keep us going when everything in us says, "I can't take any more of this." Your friendships relate to your stress level, which I'll show you in a later chapter. We all need someone cheering for us.

Eric Moussambani turned in an unforgettable performance at the 2000 Sydney Olympic Games. The twenty-two-year-old from Equatorial Guinea learned to swim only a few months before the Games. Under a special program that encourages developing countries to participate, Eric was able to enter the one-hundred-meter men's freestyle, even though he'd only practiced in a twenty-meter pool. The other two swimmers in his heat were disqualified for false starts, leaving Eric to swim alone. He flailed wildly as he swam and virtually stopped before the finish, unable to continue, until the capacity crowd jumped to their feet and cheered him on. He finally reached the wall and clung to it, having won his heat regardless, since he was the only one in the pool. Eric caught his breath then told a reporter, "It was their cheering that kept me going."[15]

What kind of support do you have? "If one falls down," says Ecclesiastes 4:10, "his friend can help him up. But pity the man who falls and has no one to help him up!" Who will help you up when you get down? Whom will you go to when you feel run down, worn out, washed up, and hopeless? *Who's in your corner?*

Strengthen the relationships you have and focus on finding the ones you need.

 Supply line #5:
Pay attention to whose voice you are listening to.

I once heard a story about an experienced spelunker who invited his friend Danny to explore a cave with him. "It's a little tough to get there," he said, "but would you like to come?" Danny, always open for a little adventure, agreed.

They entered the cavern and the passageway got smaller and smaller until both men had to walk hunched over. Pretty soon, they had to get down and crawl. Then, to Danny's horror, it got even too cramped for that. To get through a small fissure in the rock, they had to lie on their backs, push with their legs, and keep their hands to their sides. The passageway grew even narrower. They could not breathe and move at the same time. When they took a breath, their lungs expanded and filled the tiny space in the cave, causing them to get stuck. So they had to breathe out in order to move forward. Breathe in, get stuck, breathe out, push with the legs, move a tiny bit forward. How's *that* for claustrophobia? It freaks me out just to tell the story.

Danny started to lose it. *I am going to die in this cave!* he thought. *I can't go forward. I can't go back. I'm stuck!*

At that moment, Danny's friend called out to him, "Danny, this is really important. If you keep listening to those voices in your head—if you let your mind run wild—you will flip out. And if you flip out, you will get stuck in this cave. I want you to listen only to my voice right now. Danny, I have been through this, and I am here right now. I won't leave you. You can trust me. Danny, you can make it. You just have to keep listening, every moment, to my voice."

Danny died in that cave.

Just kidding! Actually, he made it all the way through, and the next cavern dazzled him beyond anything he'd ever expected to see.

What voice has your attention? Jesus says, "Keep listening to My voice. Don't listen to the voices of doubt and fear that say it's too late for you, that you should give up hope. You can trust Me. I will not leave you. I am with you always."

Pay attention to whose voice you are listening to.

Sometimes All It Takes Is Ice Cream

A young mother took her child to a restaurant. He asked if he could say grace, although he never did anything quietly. He bowed his head and prayed so loud the entire restaurant could hear him:

"God is good, God is great. Lord, I thank You for the food, and I will thank You even more when Mom gets me ice cream for dessert! And liberty and justice for all, amen."

Some customers laughed, but a cranky woman nearby said loud enough for all to hear, "Kids these days! Asking God for ice cream? He should be ashamed!"

Hearing this, the boy burst into tears and said, "Mommy? Did I do something wrong? Is God mad at me?"

As she reassured him, a gentleman approached the table. He leaned close to the kid, winked, and said, "Young man, I happen to know God. And I happen to know God thought that was a terrific prayer!"

"Really?" the boy said.

"Absolutely." Then the man nodded toward the cranky woman and said, "Too bad she doesn't ask God for ice cream. A little ice cream is good for your soul sometimes."

At the end of the meal, the mom bought her son the biggest dish of ice cream the restaurant served. His eyes lit up when it was placed in front of him. Without a word, he picked it up, walked over to the cranky lady, and said, "Here, ma'am. This is for you. A little ice cream is good for the soul sometimes. My soul's good already!"[16]

The first, most important pathway to hope is to figure out what fuels you, and then do that. Because everything in this world runs on fuel.

6.

TWO: RAISE YOUR EXPECTATIONS

With God all things are possible.

Jesus (Matthew 19:26)

Whether you think you can or whether you think you can't,
you're right.

Henry Ford

> Where there is no faith in the future,
> there is no power in the present.

In the last twelve months, I've been amazed to discover that the secular world's expectation for what could be possible seems much higher than that of people living in the Christian world. My own faith and expectations were challenged like nothing I've ever experienced when I read the 2011 authorized biography of Steve Jobs, by Walter Isaacson.[1] Steve Jobs created the Apple Corporation, was kicked out, and then returned as one of the most incredible leaders of all time. He revolutionized how the entire world experiences computers, applications, music, animation, tablet computers, and telephones.

Why? Sky-high expectations. Steve's HQ score in the area of expectations was simply off the chart. He believed impossible things could actually happen. (Many Christians don't.) He believed so strongly that obstacles could be overcome that the guys at Apple invented a term called *Steve's reality distortion field*.[2] That beats what most of us have, which is a *reality discouragement field*.

When I read his biography, I closed the book, sat back, and realized the secular business community has now started believing that impossible things are possible at the very same time the Christian community has stopped believing in the impossible. The secular world has finally discovered the power of raising their expectations at the very same time the Christian world has lowered ours. Could this be why Apple flourishes as churches decline?

Expectations matter. Great people expect more from life, and they almost always get it. You don't get what you deserve; you get what you *expect*.

The Gospel According to Steve Jobs

Steve Jobs had a habit of pushing back if an engineer or expert told him that what he wanted was impossible. An engineer once told Steve he could not suspend the law of physics. "Yes, I can," Steve said. Then, because Steve forced the people around him to find a way, they created products that the experts said could not exist, products that changed the way the world works.

Steve and his team mastered new plastics and metals for computers; then Steve focused on glass. Just before the release of the new iPhone, Steve met with his lead designer and said, "Stop production, I'm not happy with it yet." Steve determined a plastic surface looked and felt too cheap. He decided to find a durable and scratch-resistant glass that covered the front of the phone. There was a problem. A glass like that didn't exist. And he needed it fast. A friend suggested Steve call the CEO of Corning Glass, Wendell Weeks.

Getting two high-powered executives together proved to be an adventure. Steve called Corning's main switchboard and asked to speak to Weeks. An assistant told him just to fax his request to Mr. Weeks. "I'm Steve Jobs," he said. "Put me through." When she refused, Steve complained to the mutual friend about the insult. The friend told Weeks, who then called the Apple switchboard and asked to be connected to Steve. Of course, they wouldn't put Weeks through either. When Steve heard the story, he liked Weeks instantly. The two men arranged a meeting for Steve to explain to Weeks the kind of glass he needed.

"In the 1960s we developed a type of process that created something we called Gorilla Glass," Weeks said.

"Fine," Steve said. "In six months, I want enough of it to make a million iPhones."

"I'm sorry," Weeks said. He knew the request was impossible. "We've never actually *made* it. We don't even have a factory to make it."

"Don't be afraid," Steve said, looking him in the eye. "You can do it." Weeks sat looking back at Steve, incredulous. Didn't he just tell Steve it was impossible?

Steve Jobs fixed an unblinking stare at Wendell Weeks and said, "Get your mind around it. You can do this."

Weeks called in his best scientists and engineers, and placed a call to a manufacturing plant in Kentucky that was making Corning glass for LCD screens. He said, "Start the process *now* and make Gorilla Glass." Within six months, a glass that had never been created or used was the glass in six million iPhones that flooded the worldwide market.[3]

When did business executives get more faith than those who base their lives on the resurrection? When did believers in Christ stop believing that every good thing is possible? Look at what Jesus said:

- "Everything is possible for him who believes" (Mark 9:23).
- "I tell you the truth, anyone who has faith in me will do what I have been doing. He will do even greater things than these, because I am going to the Father" (John 14:12).
- "If you believe, you will receive whatever you ask for in prayer" (Matthew 21:22).

Somehow, many of us have lost that sense of believing God for the "impossible." But not everyone . . .

Nobody Votes Against a Miracle

For decades, Glen Cole, a good friend and mentor of mine, was the most significant leader in Sacramento. He was one of those who truly believed in the impossible. One day he called, and we decided to take our wives to a movie.

While driving to the movie, I asked Glen about how he had first moved to Sacramento. He said that when he arrived, someone asked why he'd come, and he answered that he was thinking about becoming the pastor of Bethel Temple. "That's the Jewish synagogue downtown, right?" the guy asked. Glen immediately knew that his potential new Christian church had a big image problem and would need to change its name.

In seminary, they tell you that a new pastor should never change anything for the first year. Who wants to risk getting thrown out of the place? But Glen told me, "Pretty soon after I arrived, we had a congregational meeting. We voted to change the name of the church, sell the church property, and move to our current location. And we hardly had any negative votes. It was practically unanimous."

"How in the world did that happen?" I asked.

"Really soon after I got there," he said, "a real estate developer from the community came to see me. He and his partners owned sixty acres on Highway 50, and he said, 'If this church decides to relocate sometime, I own land the church could buy. It would be a great location, the best in town.'"

"Then you should just give it to us," Glen said.

The man got up, left the office, and firmly closed the door behind him— all without saying a word. Glen thought, *Did I just blow the best chance of moving the church I might have had?*

The next day, the church phone rang. Glen said, "The same man who had walked out the day before said, 'It's yours.' And I said, 'Hallelujah!'"

Glen called the congregational meeting, at which the church changed its name to Capital Christian Center, voted to sell its property and then move to the sixty acres, where it would build a church facility and a school.

With a twinkle in his eye, Glen said, "The vote was unanimous, because nobody votes against a miracle."

But that didn't finish our conversation that night. Glen fired up a bit. (Nothing is better than being with a seventy-eight-year-old who is fully alive!) He said, "Do you know what's wrong with the church these days? *Nobody believes miracles can happen anymore.* We need to get back to the days where we actually think it's possible that miracles can happen. The church is going to be dead and lifeless until we start believing that impossible things are possible."[4]

I told you in chapter 2 about Hilda, the amazing leader at Dandora Baptist Church in Kenya. Everyone around her saw the unfinished church in terms of what it was right then. They didn't think it could change. There was no hope. The economy was bad. They didn't have money. They didn't have resources. They just didn't have what it takes. But one woman stood in a church with her shoes off, praying, because she expected God to act. Today, that church has three hundred school kids housed in a finished building. Hilda's expectations triggered hope that fueled something that was, to that community, nothing short of miraculous.

To raise your HQ, raise your expectations. You will never create a new telephone, invent new glass, raise the hopes of a church, build a facility for three hundred children in one of the worst slums in Africa, or raise the hopes of a family, a marriage, a career, or another person, until your expectations are raised. You will never lift the hopes of a city, a family, a career, or another person until your expectations are raised. Your hope level only rises when your expectations are elevated.

The rest of this chapter will explain five attitudes and actions that will help you become a person who expects great things.

Trait #1—Believe Impossible Things Are Possible

Everyone has heard, "You get what you deserve." It's not true. You actually get what you *expect*. Jesus was clear about this.

In the second chapter of Mark, we read about four vision-filled friends who had a huge expectation. They thought that if they could get their sick buddy to Jesus, He could make something impossible happen. Their expectations rose so high, they grabbed their friend, carried him to the house where Jesus was teaching, and when they realized the crowd was too thick to get through, sawed a hole in the roof of the home and lowered their friend down to Jesus. Their expectation led to action and to a miracle when Jesus completely healed their friend.

The story of these four guys suggests to me that if your expectations are high enough, it's even possible to trigger a miracle. They didn't *cause* a miracle. That's God's job. However, their expectations led to actions that triggered God *doing* a miracle. Why would you want to live any other way, when you know your actions can trigger a miracle in your life and in the lives of others around you?

On the other hand, I believe the most depressing, debilitating acronym ever is *TWNC*: *Things Will Never Change*. This toxic, dangerous thought process has the power to destroy your marriage, friendships, and career.

These four words, *Things Will Never Change*, replace confidence with cynicism.

These four words, *Things Will Never Change*, replace high hopes with depression and despair.

These four words, *Things Will Never Change*, blind people to the possibility that God might have better days ahead.

These four words, *Things Will Never Change*, are so powerful they can handcuff the hands of God. Jesus didn't do any miracles in His hometown of Nazareth. Why? The Bible says, "because of their unbelief" (Matthew 13:58 NKJV).

We've become less like Steve Jobs and more like most car companies. Have you ever seen a concept car unveiled at an auto show? They *rock*! But when you see what comes out five years later, you say, "That *reeks*." How did they snatch defeat from the jaws of victory? What typically happens is that the engineers say *this* is impossible and the finance people say *that* is impossible, and by the time they're done, they've created a goofy car that nobody wants.

Start believing impossible things are possible, because you're going to get what you *expect*.

Trait #2—Believe That God Has Better Days Ahead

More than sixty years ago, a small town in Maine disappeared under the waves when a utility company built a dam on the Dead River. Flooding started in 1949, but it took three years to submerge the homes, streets, and memories. When the utility decided to build the dam, a representative went to each resident and said in essence, "We're building a huge dam at the end of this valley, and water is going to back up and fill the whole area. We'll pay you for your property and you can live here for free until you have to move, but at some point, your town is going to be submerged, so you'll have to move."

About a year after the utility company bought the property, a writer revisited what had been his family's home. It was now a town with an expiration date. Many of the residents hadn't yet moved away, but he saw a remarkable change in the town.

What was once a charming neighborhood of tidy homes with fenced yards had become a dilapidated ghost town. Why repair a blown-down fence when it was going to be knocked over by a wave anyway? Why fix a window or a pothole? Why try to be neighborly if everyone was moving away?

Then he penned this incredible summary line: "Where there is no faith in the future, there is no power in the present."[5]

Men and women with high HQs uniformly believe that better days lie ahead. They expect positive things to happen and work to make those things happen. They expect to see good things ahead instead of fearing imminent disaster. No one washes a rental car or rearranges hotel room furniture before they check out. No one invests more money or works out harder when they expect everything to go south. Where there is no faith in the future, there is no power in the present.

Trait #3—Realize the Power of Perspective

A young college student wrote her parents a tough letter during her sophomore year. She said,

Dear Mom and Dad,

I know this is really going to be disappointing to you, but I met a guy. He's about fifteen years older than I am. We're in love. We just eloped. I'm two months pregnant. I'm dropping out of school and I will contact you at some point in the future. I'm really sorry,

Your Daughter

Just below the note she added a "P.S." instructing her mom and dad to turn over the letter. On the back, it said:

Just kidding. But I did flunk one class and I need two hundred dollars. Please keep this in perspective.

Most of us are waiting on a change of circumstances, but what we really need is a change in *perspective*. Often, it's not low circumstances that make us lose hope—it's low expectations. No one knows this better than a bunch of old-timers in Green Bay, Wisconsin.

Back in the 1940s and 50s, the Green Bay Packers were an atrocious football team. For eleven years they only won 28 percent of their games. (That means they *lost* more than 70 percent of the time!) In 1958, they had an embarrassing one win and ten losses, the worst record in Packers history. All that was about to change.

On February 2, 1959, Vince Lombardi stepped in as coach and leader of the Green Bay Packers, and they experienced their first winning season in more than a decade. Rookie head coach Lombardi was named Coach of the Year. The next nine years were nine winning seasons. Now they had *won* more than 70 percent of their games. They claimed five national championships, including the first two Super Bowls.

What happened? What turned a losing team with eleven years of failure into the most winning team for nine years in a row? What took a group of discouraged, dispirited athletes and turned them into champions? What changed everything for the Green Bay Packers? Simple. One person arrived and brought with him a completely different perspective and higher expectations.

We see this principle all over the Bible. Jerusalem was a disaster. What's worse, nothing had gotten better for ninety-two years. Nehemiah showed up there, in a city that had a scorecard that looked like this:

Years since the city wall was destroyed	92
Years the people were stuck there	92
Years of failure	92
Years of broken dreams	92

For ninety-two years, the "walled" city of Jerusalem had no walls, and its people lived under the control of what I call the Four F's—fear, failure, frustration, and fatigue. Then *one guy* arrived with a perspective not of what *had been* but of what it *could become*. After Nehemiah got there, the scorecard looked like this:

Number of days to rebuild the wall	52
Done. Game over.	

In just fifty-two days the people rebuilt a wall that they themselves had said for ninety-two years couldn't be built. What changed? One guy arrived with raised expectations and the city was forever changed.

When you are the person who arrives on the scene with the right perspective and higher expectations, everything can change.

Trait #4—Replace FEAR with FAITH

One of the clearest examples of how to replace fear with faith involves an expectant young David and a fearful nation of Israel (1 Samuel 17). You know the story of David and Goliath, how a young Hebrew shepherd defeated a giant Philistine warrior using only a sling and some small stones. The people expected nothing but defeat. David expected nothing but victory. The people thought Goliath was too big to beat. David thought he was too big to miss.

The people of Israel weren't filled with expectation. They were filled with fear. There's a definition of fear I like to use: *fear is the darkroom where negatives develop.* Israel allowed four destructive steps—FEAR—to keep it quivering on the sidelines. But David made five positive choices—FAITH—to take a risk for God. The steps on the left always lead to a spiral of defeat. The choices on the right spiral us ever upward into action and victory.

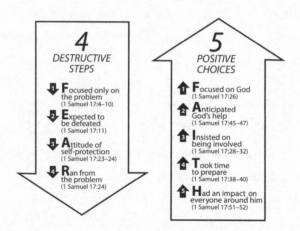

Every person is going to live on the left side or the right side. The side they live on determines their expectation level. Most people want their lives to change. The most powerful way to have a rapid life change is not to wait for circumstances to change but to move from FEAR to FAITH (see diagram).

Now skip to the end of the David and Goliath story in your mind. When do the people quit whining and stop being afraid? When do they rise up, shout, charge, and go to battle? After one guy with raised expectations had the courage to act. David changed *everything* for his nation when he moved from the left column to the right, from fear to a powerful faith.

Living on the fear side of the page is prison. Moving to the faith side of the page is freedom. It's a constant battle, but it's one that you and I just have to win. I've probably preached this very lesson to myself thirty times in the last four months, and three thousand times overall.

At our first meeting to launch Bayside twenty years ago, about twenty-five people showed up. I walked out of that meeting thinking, *I doubt this church is going to get off the ground.* That was the height of my expectation. But my partner in this new endeavor, Dave Olson, saw something different that night. With a spring in his step and a gleam in his eye, he walked out saying, "I think God is up to something special here, and we need to stay at it!"

That was almost twenty years ago. Dave was right; I was wrong. He had a divine expectation; I had a human fear. He saw better days ahead; I had to take my blinders off.

Am I glad I did. And you'll be glad, too, when you start looking to the future with great expectation. Whatever you need, God is greater. Whatever you're going through, God is bigger. Whatever your weakness, God is stronger. Raise your expectation of what God can do. Raise your expectation of what He will do with you. Replace your FEAR with FAITH.

Trait #5—Replace "What If?" with "Why Not?"

> *While theoretically and technically television may be feasible, commercially and financially it is an impossibility, a development which we need waste little time dreaming.*
>
> LEE DE FOREST, INVENTOR OF
> THE CATHODE RAY TUBE, 1926[6]

I think there is a world market for maybe five computers.

THOMAS J. WATSON, IBM

CHAIRMAN OF THE BOARD, 1943[7]

Airplanes are interesting toys but of no military value.

MARSHAL FERDINAND FOCH, FAMED

WORLD WAR I MILITARY STRATEGIST, 1904[8]

With over 50 foreign cars already on sale here, the Japanese auto industry isn't likely to carve out a big slice of the U.S. market.

Businessweek, 1958[9]

Stocks have reached what looks like a permanently high plateau.

IRVING FISHER, ECONOMIST,

OCTOBER 16, 1929[10]

We don't think the Beatles will do anything in their market. Guitar groups are on their way out.

RECORDING COMPANY EXPERT, 1962[11]

A friend named Roger Crawford has mastered the art of "what if" versus "why not." Roger was born with four shortened limbs, including two misshapen hands that protrude from his forearms with two fingers on one and one on the other. An amputation put him on an artificial leg. Everybody but his parents told him, "Roger, you're never going to be able to *blah blah blah blah.*" And yet Roger learned to play tennis. He not only learned to play, he became an NCAA Division I tennis champion and went on to become a United States Professional Tennis Association athlete. *Sports Illustrated* calls him "one of the most accomplished physically challenged athletes in the world."[12]

Roger speaks to audiences all over the world, urging them to prove critics and doubt pushers wrong. He speaks of "turning the pessimism of 'I can't' into the unstoppable power of 'I can!'" As a boy, he could have let his imagination whisper, *If only you had been born with normal legs and feet! It isn't fair!*

You might as well be realistic about this. Instead, he trained his imagination to wonder, *What if you learned to play tennis? Wouldn't that be cool? Wouldn't it be fun to watch the face of some arrogant jerk when he sees a guy with one leg and no hands beat the pants off him?*

The US government invited Roger to visit Walter Reed Memorial Hospital in Washington, DC, to walk through the wards and talk to soldiers who had limbs blown off in combat. Roger said it felt unbelievably depressing. One after another, he saw the devastating results of war. Then he walked up to a young man who lay flat on his back, unable to move.

"How are you doing?" Roger said. The guy had a big smile on his face. It turned out he was a committed Christian.

"Hey, you don't have normal arms either," the patient said. "How can I pray for *you*?"

The question blew Roger away. After they talked a bit, this newly disabled young soldier said, "I'm going to walk again, just like you."

"What's your secret?" Roger said. "Everybody in here is devastated and depressed, and you actually have hope."

"I'm flat on my back," the young soldier said, "so the only thing I can do is look up."

"You know what?" Roger said. "If you can look up, you can get up."[13]

Raise your expectations and your hopes will begin to soar. Because when you look up, you will get up.

7.

THREE: REFOCUS ON THE FUTURE

One thing I do, forgetting what is behind, I look forward to what is ahead.

PHILIPPIANS 3:13; AUTHOR'S PARAPHRASE

Beware of spending too much time looking back at what you once were when God wants you to become something you have never been.

OSWALD CHAMBERS

Ever get halfway through something and suddenly realize, *This was a really bad idea*? A couple of friends and I were out waterskiing when the wind kicked up. The lake went from calm and serene to choppy and dangerous. One of my buddies (the least bright) said, "I know! Let's play a game called suicide!" The rest of us (i.e., the victims) said, "Okay!" We shortened the towrope to about fifteen feet and got the boat going as fast as possible. The minute the skier was ready, somebody would click a stopwatch to signal the boat driver, "Game on." How long could you stay up—in choppy water—behind a speeding boat—with a driver whose only goal was to make you fall? That was the game.

Thirty seconds into my turn, I was flying as fast as I'd ever gone. The driver whipped me out to the right, trying to throw me over. Right then, ten feet ahead of me, I saw a duck. I skied right at it. Normally when you get that close to ducks, they dive underwater (that's why they're called *ducks*). But as I began to bear down on this duck, the duck didn't move. At the last second, I put my ski to the inside and went ripping past this obstinate bird. I thought, *Why didn't this dumb duck duck?* And then I saw what was right behind this *mom* duck—several little baby ducklings.

Do you know how random thoughts can sprint through your brain really fast (especially during history class)? My first thought was, *What an awesome mom! She seemed to say, "You ain't messin' with* my *kids!"* Then, *Isn't that just like God? He shelters us.* And then, *The guys in the boat have to see this.*

"Check this out!" I yelled, while looking back at the mom duck and her ducklings. I was so caught up by the scene that I forgot what I was doing—namely, skiing in choppy water at about forty miles per hour, fifteen feet behind a boat controlled by crazy guys trying to make sure I would fall.

I never saw it coming. The wake. Both skis came to an abrupt halt when they went under it, and I was yanked right out of them. Looking back had so disoriented me that as I slammed into the water, I forgot to let go of the rope. For several seconds, I got pulled underwater at high speed.

I finally let go.

With the wind knocked out of me, I surfaced and checked for broken ribs, followed by a frantic search for my swim trunks. My buddies were laughing so hard they practically fell off the boat. I learned an important lesson that day.

Nobody ever goes forward well when they are looking back.

I have one goal in this chapter. I want to ask you one question that has the power to change the rest of your life. This one question is so important it should be the primary question asked by every parent of every teenager. This question is so important it should be the primary question asked by a spouse discouraged by his or her marriage. This question is so important it should be asked by anyone currently feeling discouraged about themselves. This question is so important it should be the first question asked by people who want to change their lives, lose weight, get out of debt, or have a better future. This question has the power to lift a person out of discouragement. It has the power to transform somebody's mood. It has the power to turn around a company or a church or a family.

This question is actually more than a question.

It becomes a frame of reference for how you look at everything. When this question moves from being a question to being a habit, to being your lifestyle, everybody you know will be affected. A person trained to ask this question becomes

- someone people flock to for advice and encouragement,
- the parent everybody wishes they had,
- the spouse everybody wishes they were married to,
- the friend everybody wishes they knew, and
- a better person, a better coach, a better teacher, a better employee, a better leader.

This question is the reason Peter went from being a complete failure to being one of the first great leaders of the Christian church. I believe this question was uppermost in Jesus' mind every time He looked at His disciples.

Here is the question:

What can this become?

We learn this from Jesus. Jesus tipped His hand when He looked at some young, inexperienced men and made an astounding statement: "Follow Me, and I will make you *become* fishers of men" (Mark 1:17 NASB, emphasis added).

None of the disciples was a first-round draft pick. They were a mess. Peter had his mouth always open, his foot always in it. Thomas met every plan with, "I doubt it." St. John the Divine? That same John and his brother James were called the "Sons of Thunder." Matthew was a selfish tax collector. As a group, they were always arguing about who was greatest. The only thing they seemed to do right was "borrow" a kid's lunch one day so Jesus could feed five thousand people.

What made Jesus so effective? What made Him the single most magnetic leader ever to walk this planet? What was it about Jesus that liberated people from their pasts and freed them to go on to become something they never dreamed?

Here it is:

Jesus was not focused on what people were like.

He was focused on what they could become.

Show me a parent of a teenager who is focused on what their kid is like right now, and I'll show you a discouraged parent. Show me a parent who is focused on what his or her teenager can become, and anything is possible.

Show me a husband or wife focused on what his or her marriage is like right now, and usually I can show you a discouraged person. Show me a couple focused on what their marriage can become, and anything is possible.

Show me Christians focused on what their spiritual lives are like right now. In all likelihood they will be discouraged, but the minute they begin to focus on what their relationship with God could become, anything is possible.

Show me a person who wishes he was in better shape physically but is focused on what his life is like right now, and he is probably discouraged. Yet all kinds of possibilities emerge the minute he focuses on what he could become in the future.

Everything changes when we ask the question, "Am I able to see things not as they *are right now* but in terms of what they can *become*?"

"I will make you *become* fishers of men," Jesus said, and by following through on His word, He changed, is changing, and will change the world. Forever.

Become Versus Is

During the process of writing this book, I had a conversation with one of the sharpest Christian leaders I've ever come across. Brilliant, fun, enjoyable to be with, he also has a track record of great God-honoring successes. As we got to know each other, he described the typical parent's frustration of trying to help his stepson stop spiraling in negative directions. Nothing he tried had worked. Both he and his stepson felt discouraged, beat up, and angry. He knew I had worked a lot with teenagers and asked, "What can I try that hasn't already failed?" Great question!

There aren't any magic formulas, I told him, but several years ago, I learned a lifesaving lesson. I still consider this the single healthiest psychological discipline I've ever discovered for improving toxic situations. I told this stepfather that the minute I begin to spiral into discouragement over the way something is, *I remind myself to ask the right question.*

"The starting point is this," I said. "If you continue to see your stepson as he is right now, you both will be locked into a prison of discouragement. However, if you can begin to see him in terms of what he can *become*, and you begin to pray and think toward that end, it opens up all kinds of potential for the two of you. It may not change your stepson right away, but it will change you and liberate you from the kind of discouragement people feel when they look backward."

Two weeks later, I received a call from that dad. I'd love to say his son's life was turned around, he became a straight-A student, and he now comes home every day and says, "Father, what chores could I help with around the house?" The dad didn't say that, but he did say that one phrase has liberated him, has changed the atmosphere of his home, and has started to change his relationship with his stepson. What can the son *become*?

When I stop looking at the way things are and instead start to see them for what they can become, everything changes. I don't know anything as powerful as this simple practice for replacing discouragement with encouragement. Asking the question creates a new future. It changes the way I do life. It alters the way I view my past. It revamps the way I approach my Christian faith. When we focus on what something can *become*, we come alive.

Meet Prof

In February 2013, the Christian world lost a spiritual giant. Howard G. Hendricks died at age ninety after decades of teaching this generation's greatest communicators. "Prof," as he was called, taught Christian education at

Dallas Seminary for more than half a century and put his inimitable stamp on many of the most influential leaders of our day, including Chuck Swindoll, Tony Evans, Bruce Wilkinson, David Jeremiah, and countless others.

A decade before his passing, the *Dallas Morning News* published a sparkling profile of his great influence and notable accomplishments. It suggested that no other educator has influenced the evangelical world like Hendricks. David Jeremiah said of him, "Impact is only as good as it plays out in future generations. Prof is like a pebble thrown in a lake—the ripples just keep going outward."[1]

Hendricks taught students, but even more, he helped students see what they could *become*. In his commentary on the gospel of Mark, Swindoll wrote,

> When I was in seminary, I took a course from many great men. One of them was Dr. Howard Hendricks. Every once in a while, he would write an affirming note at the top of my paper. One time he wrote, "This is great, Chuck. Someday you will write." Years later, as I put together my first book, those words fueled my drive to get the manuscript done. The words, "Someday you will write," freed me to write.[2]

And Chuck did write, with millions of copies of books now in print. "Prof" planted that idea of what Chuck could *become*.

Howard Hendricks, though, would not have become "Prof" without Miss Noe. His parents split up right after his birth and his grandmother raised him. He described himself as "a troublemaker, a hell-raiser." His fifth-grade teacher, Miss Simon, once tied him to his chair with a rope, taping his mouth shut. She predicted that Howard, whom she called "the worst behaved child in this school," would end up in prison, along with four of his classmates. Three of them proved her right.

When the next school year began, his sixth-grade teacher, Miss Noe, went down the roll and called out his name, then looked up, only to see him sitting with his arms folded, "just waiting to go into action." She studied him for a moment and said, "I've heard a lot about you." Howard said he immediately thought, *Here we go again*. She smiled and added, "but I don't believe a word of it!"

The words stunned him. Hendricks said that Miss Noe made him realize, for the first time, that someone cared. Hendricks called that moment "a fundamental turning point, not only in my education, but in my life. Suddenly, unexpectedly, someone believed in me. For the first time in my life, someone saw potential in me." In previous years, he had skipped assignments, but now he stayed up until one in the morning to do special assignments for Miss Noe. Fifth grade had been the worst year of his life. Sixth grade became the best. Miss Noe called out what Howard could *become*.[3] In future years, Prof did the same with thousands of his own students.

Why does asking this one question change everything?

- When a teacher focuses on what a student can *become*, rather than on what he or she is, the future is liberated from the past.
- When a business focuses on what it can *become*, rather than on what it has been, new and exciting opportunities can be pursued.
- When a church focuses on what it can *become*, rather than on what it is, fresh vision can finally lead to a better future.
- When an out-of-shape weekend warrior focuses on what he can *become*, rather than on what he is, he will finally have energy to get into shape.

In other words, when we finally start focusing on what something or someone can *become*, rather than on what or who it is, *everything changes.*

I have four kids. All amazing, none perfect. Like kids of all ages, including their dad, there were times when things didn't go well. If you were to ask my daughter Christy what I usually said after they pulled some stunt we didn't agree with, she would answer, "He says, 'That's just not like you.'" All four kids would say the same.

"That's just not like you" is a phrase I value like pure gold. When my kids were growing up, I realized that if they defined themselves as they were, or worse, what others said they were, instead of staying focused on what they could *become*, we would all be in for a miserable time.

On occasion, I connect with a teenager who is heading in destructive directions. A parent will say, "My teenager is hanging out with a really bad crowd and is going downhill fast!" I met with a kid just like that two weeks ago at a Peet's coffee shop.

"You know," I said, "I really don't care what you're doing right now. Your parents care a lot, but I don't. Here's my question for you: What do you want to *become*? Is this the type of person you *really want to become*? Will the road you're on right now get you to where you want to *be*?"

It is never sudden or easy, but the road away from destructive directions *always* starts by getting someone liberated from what they are like right now.

"What can this become?" is the *only* question that leads a person to catch fresh vision. If you want people to have a better future, then help them focus on what things can *become*, not on what they are now. Fresh vision comes by asking, *What can I become? What can this become? What can he or she become? What can our marriage become?*

The answer to the question is *always* fresh vision. Fresh vision leads to encouragement. Encouragement leads to hope. Hope leads to change. Change leads to better days ahead. The benefits to asking this question are limitless. I'll share with you some of the most important benefits.

▲ Benefit #1—Passion Replaces Apathy and Discouragement

Robert Fulghum wrote some of my favorite books, including *All I Really Need to Know I Learned in Kindergarten*[4] (which, unfortunately, I read after spending thousands of dollars on graduate school). One time when I heard him speak, he said, "Find any group of children and ask them how many can sing, and what happens? Every hand goes up. I ask, 'What can you sing?' and they answer, 'Everything!' 'What if you don't know the words?' 'We'll make them up!' Find any group of kids, ask them, 'How many of you can draw?' and everybody's hand goes up."

But what happens when you ask that same group of kids the same questions twenty-five years later? How many can sing? Almost none of them. How many can draw? No hands go up. Fulghum asks a profound question: "What happened? What happened between kindergarten and adulthood to stomp out that God-given spark of passion that God placed in every single kid, so that by the time they become adults, the fire's gone out? What happened to the spark?"

I'm sure you've seen it happen. A marriage started aflame, but seven years later they're just waiting for the last spark to flicker out. New Christians are fired up and passionate about their faith; three years later they treat the gospel as old, cold news. Churches start with fresh passion and momentum but decline into apathetic indifference. Everybody is all-in for a new start-up, but five years after the launch coworkers argue and fight over titles, policy, procedure, position, and the corner office.

Is it possible to get that passion back? Can you reignite the flame, rediscover the spark, and regain momentum? Yes. Passion, hope, and momentum all return when people begin asking, "Regardless of what I see now—what can this *become*?" That single shift reignites passion, creates new energy, and sets people on fire again to do something great in their world.

▲ Benefit #2—You Experience Great Comebacks

Every great comeback in history began with fresh vision. It's not where you start—it's what you *become*.

- *Jonah* started out running away from God but ended up influencing a whole metropolis.
- *Thomas* started out wracked by doubt but ended up taking the gospel all the way to India.
- *Moses* did nothing significant for the first two-thirds of his life—which I find encouraging—but ended up delivering two million people from centuries of slavery.
- *Jacob* started out as a liar and ended up becoming a leader.
- *Timothy* started out shy, fearful, and insecure but ended up becoming the apostle Paul's protégé.

- *Paul* started out persecuting Christians but ended up writing the majority of the New Testament.
- *John Mark* started out as a quitter but ended up tapped by the Spirit of God to paint a portrait of Jesus Christ.
- *Peter* started out as an arrogant loudmouth who threw Jesus under a bus but ended up as a great Christian leader.

Again, it's not where you start—it's what you become. When a parent focuses on what a child can *become*, that parent becomes far more encouraged and far more encouraging. When leaders in a business focus on what it can *become*, rather than on its failures, those leaders can carve out an exciting new future for the company.

Back in 2002, a slumping Reuters recorded losses of almost 500 million pounds, prompting its CEO to describe the company as "fighting for survival." Only one year later, however, it recorded *profits* of almost 500 million pounds.[5] How did the leadership manage this astonishing turnaround? They stopped focusing on what *was* and instead reimagined what the company *could be*, and then they took decisive action to make that fresh vision a reality.

My dad was a successful businessman. I'd been a Christian for about two years when he came to me one day and said, "Jon Archer thinks a lot of you."

"What do you mean?" I said. Jon Archer's dad had written books for Billy Graham and now Jon was pastoring the church I was attending.

"I really don't want to see you doing this church stuff," he said. "I'd rather see you in business or sports. But Jon told me, 'I think your son could become a Christian leader that would impact people in ways he could never imagine now.'"

As a college student, I'd been watching Christian friends of mine and thinking, *I don't even know the Bible. All these Christians are on top of things, and I'm just this little spiritual peon.* I'll never forget that conversation. It astonished me that Jon Archer saw something in me that I couldn't see at all. He didn't see what I *was* but what I could *become*.

All of us need to hang around individuals who believe we can become far more than we ourselves think is possible. More on that in chapter 9, which you're going to *love*.

⬆ Benefit #3—Grace Frees You; Future Vision Fuels You

Grace frees us from the chains of the past. Vision fuels us to reach something better out ahead. Grace helps us change tracks from what was to what could be. Vision supplies the energy to reach the great destination at a distance down the tracks.

Some people get *freed* but not *fueled*. For some, the hurts and disappointments of the past no longer hold them, yet they meander through life, not too excited about anything.

Other people are *fueled* but not *freed*. They have great ideas and a strong passion to see them take shape, but remembering their pasts keeps them anchored in place.

When someone finally focuses on what they can become, they're free. Hope replaces guilt, and encouragement overpowers discouragement. With the chains off, we start dreaming about a far better future, a future we can now start to build. And when I say *dream*, I mean dream *big*.

One of our mottos at Bayside Church is "Come, fail, but for God's sake, try *something*." Why insult God by dreaming up really small plans?

Groups of various kinds often ask me to help reinvigorate whatever it is they do and reset vision for them. I'll put 80 to 120 people in a room and keep them working together for up to two days. I seat them in small groups and ask things like, "What are you going to do to reach your community? What are you going to do to unleash compassion? What are you going to do to help your people grow spiritually? What are you going to do to develop your leaders? If somebody took the handcuffs off you, what would you just *love* to see happen?"

Everybody works individually and writes down ideas, and then each table discusses those ideas. Eventually, each table gets to announce seven or so ideas to the whole group, and I write them all down. It's an absolute blast. I stand back and see life come into the room, in living color. Asking "What can this become?" points the way to a new future and fills people with healthy passion.

Right after I became a Christian, I walked into the boardroom of a vibrant church and saw a sign hanging on the wall. It said, "Money flows best not to needy institutions but to bold goals and exciting ideas." I still remember it, four decades later. Why become something timid and pale when you can become something alive and vibrant?

Benefit #4—You Are Set Free to Dream!

Years ago, I learned that people fall into five categories:[6]

1. Those with no dream

Many of us have only one goal in life: to make it through the day. I once heard Chuck Swindoll describe a conversation with a college student. He asked the young man what was meant to be a profound question: "Where are you headed?"

"To lunch," the kid said.

For a lot of people, that's the whole dream.

Not having a dream results in three unhealthy emotions: frustration, boredom, and regret. Frustration, because if you don't set goals, you move through life from crisis to crisis. Without a dream for your life, you're a reactor, not an actor. Boredom, because you have nothing to shoot for and nothing powerful to capture your interest. Without a dream, you move from diversion to diversion, and they all get old sooner rather than later. Regret, because you will tend to say, "If only I'd done this" or "If only I'd done that." That's tragic, because we all have the freedom to choose.

2. Those with a low dream

Some dreams provide no real challenge because they're just not big enough. These people end up settling or selfish. They settle for a life without God-honoring, world-impacting dreams. Or their dreams are all self-centered. When people tell me, "My dream is to make a lot of money and then retire,"

I think, *When's the last time you saw a U-Haul following a hearse?* Life is too short and your potential for impact is too great to build a self-centered life or settle for small dreams.

(X) 3. Those with the wrong dream

I see people all around me, in our church and community, with tremendous talent, ability, and potential, yet they give first-class allegiance to second-class causes. One day we will stand before the Lord and He will say, "What did you do with your life? What did you do with the gifts, talents, and resources I gave you?"

Unworthy causes can be religious as well as nonreligious. I once met with a sharp Christian who was working very hard to make a church in his denomination keep the name of the denomination in the name of the church. After about thirty minutes I said, "Now, understand this. I like your denomination. I speak at a lot of your churches. A lot of pastors coming to our Thrive Leadership Conferences are your pastors. And I want to tell you that you are way too smart to give your life to this. There is a world of great need and you could save lives, restore hope, rescue marriages, develop teenagers, reach kids . . ." He was a world-class guy who wanted to give his life to a second-class cause. Get this one! Don't give first-class allegiance to second-class causes.

(?) 4. Those with a vague dream

Vague dreams are unclear, unfocused, misty. The only dreams that take shape in the real world and change it for the better are those with a razor-sharp focus. Jesus Christ knew what He was about. As Reggie Ogea notes, "When Jesus Christ was only twelve years old, He knew his purpose in life." He told His parents, "I must be about My Father's business" (Luke 2:49 NKJV). At the end of His life, He said, "It is finished" (John 19:30). You can't say, "It is finished" unless you know exactly where you have to go. Ogea concluded, "Many a person journeys through life without ever clarifying and defining his dreams."[7]

Is a dream percolating in you? If so, how sharp and clear does it look?

🔼 5. Those with God's dream

People with a God-inspired dream know where they're headed, because the Word of God, the Spirit inside them, and the believers they trust all point them in the same direction. How do you know if the dream inside you really comes from God? The answer to that question would take a whole book to unpack, but three good questions can reveal a lot:

1. Is this dream God-honoring?
2. Will this dream change lives and influence people?
3. Does this dream resonate with godly, visionary people?

I met with a young pastor last week who has a dream that every school in his town will have a sponsoring church. These churches will make sure that each kid has every resource he or she needs to thrive at school. The churches will tutor kids, assist in classrooms, give money, build facilities, and support in any way needed. They are committed to ensuring every facility is equipped and every faculty has what they need to maximize the educational experience of every student. He is committed that in his community "No School Will Be Left Behind."

This pastor had that same passion in his eyes and the same energy in his ministry that happens to *every* person who has a God-honoring dream.

🔼 Benefit #5—Forward Momentum Stabilizes and Energizes

Asking the question "What can I *become?*" energizes and stabilizes. I occasionally do things at church that might get most pastors fired. A while ago, our ministry team dreamed up a great way to make a point about how forward momentum stabilizes your life. That Sunday, we had a bike race around the auditorium, with the prize going to the person who finished *last.* The problem is, riding a bike slowly is a lot harder than riding it fast. A slow-moving bike is less stable than a bike staying still. Forward motion results in stability.

Asking "What can this *become*?" accelerates you to the kind of fresh vision that fuels forward motion. Asking what things can *become* gives you hope *and* a future.

If you feel discouraged or dejected about your life, or if you desire to move to a higher level of living now or in the future, no strategy is more powerful than to focus on what you can *become* rather than on what you *are*.

Do your future a big favor. Give preference to *become* over *is*. The future you will thank you for it.

The rest of us will thank you, too, because we all need your gifts and talents, as you'll see in the next chapter.

8.

FOUR: PLAY TO YOUR STRENGTHS

In his grace, God has given us different gifts for doing certain things well.

ROMANS 12:6 NLT

Your talent is God's gift to you. What you do with it is your gift back to God.

LEO BUSCAGLIA

In an old joke, people refer to seminary as *cemetery*. Attending one does feel like that at times, so the last thing I expected to discover in a dingy classroom in the basement of a Pasadena seminary some years ago was something huge. It changed the course of my life. The professor went off script that day and woke up our class by asking some urgent questions:

- Do you want to have a life that is one level above the boring existence lived by the vast majority of people?
- Do you want to live in such a way that when you get to the end of your life you have few regrets?
- Do you want to make a maximum impact with the one life you get to live?
- Do you want to have a life where God actually uses you to change things?

- Do you want to have a life that is exciting, fulfilling, exhilarating, and occasionally terrifying, but where you actually really matter?
- Do you want a life where you are more encouraged and less discouraged?

He closed with this dramatic statement: "All that and more will happen if you do *this one thing* . . .

"Play to your strengths."

Then, like any good professor, he emphasized and expanded it. "Find out what your spiritual gifts are; then build your entire life around them. Anything else is going to take you down the road to misery and mediocrity."

With that one thought, my professor changed the course of my life. I have never recovered. Let me give you seven reasons why.

Reason #1—Discovering Your God-Given Gifts Helps You Maximize Your Potential

Think about world-class consultants for giant corporations. Consultants meet with their clients and say, "We're going to think deeply about how your company can maximize its potential." Next, they ask their first question: "What can your company be the best in the world at?" Then they say, "That's the starting point for reaching your maximum potential."

The same is true with individuals. What can you be the one best in the world at? Try a quick experiment. Write your name on the line below, next to mine.

_____   *Ray Johnston*

Now switch hands and write it again. See the difference?

_____   *Ray Johnston*

Here's the point of the experiment. If you don't take time to discover, develop, and use the gifts God has given you, then you will spend your entire life writing with the wrong hand.

You can live on the minimum, traveling down a road to misery and mediocrity, which is what you can expect if you leave the tremendous gifts God has placed within you undiscovered and unused. Or you can follow the professor's advice. Discovering and deploying your God-given gifts is the key to identifying your purpose in life and maximizing your potential.

Reason #2—Discovering Your God-Given Gifts Helps You Discover Your Purpose

When you identify and start using your God-given gifts, you will feel a surge of hope rise within you. That's just the way God set it up. Many surveys show that most people are in the wrong job. Think they might deal with a little hopelessness?

The average American lives 28,708 days,[1] yet most people never take even one day to figure out why they're here. Knowing your God-given gifts will answer questions like, "What does God want me to do with my life?" "What should my mission be?" "Why am I here?" "How do I make a maximum impact?" The really important questions in life clear up as you discover your God-given gifts. God would not give you those gifts if He did not want you to use them.

Most people don't even have to change jobs or retrain for a new career for their hopes to soar. They just need to find a place, even outside of the workplace, to start exercising their gifts. We all come fully alive when we discover our gifts, put the gifts into service, and then watch as God works powerfully through them (1 Corinthians 12:4–6). The second we take our gifts and put them into service, *wham*! God shows up and works as only He can.

Reason #3—Discovering Your God-Given Gifts Helps Free You from Insecurity and Inferiority

I have something really important to tell you. You are gifted by God.

I asked people at church one Sunday, "Raise your hand if you think you're really gifted." A few hands went up. Then I taught a series on "Discovering and Developing Your God-Given Gifts." By the end of the series my goal was to ask the question again and see every hand in the air. *Why?* Because the Bible is crystal clear: every person matters, every gift God gave you matters, and each person's gift is equally important.

There's a great story about a woman shouting at her son who was hiding under the bed on a Sunday morning, crying, refusing to go to their church that had been having some problems.

"Come out this minute!" the woman shouted. "You're ruining your suit!"

"I don't care about my suit," the son said.

"You have to go to church!"

"Tell me one good reason," the son said.

"I'll tell you three! Because people are depending on you, because it honors God, and because you're the pastor."

Perhaps that church just didn't have enough people using their God-given gifts. Is the pastor's gift the most important on any given Sunday? What about the gifted person who remembers the key to open the church doors? What about the gifted teenager who turns on the microphone? No congregation could "do church" without gifted people who are rarely seen. Without gifted people guiding traffic in the parking lot, we'd have accidents. Without gifted people paying the electric bill, doing graphic arts for advertising, or setting up chairs, we'd all stand awkwardly alone in the dark.

A revival took place in a North Carolina tent back in 1934. Two fourteen-year-old boys walked up to the tent, looked around, heard the music, and quickly identified it as a church service. They turned around and started to leave when an usher approached them and said, "Young men, you might like this. We have some seats over there." He led them to two open seats. A little-known speaker named Mordecai Ham spoke that night, a man who never got a book deal, a television program, or an invitation to the White House. Nobody names their kid after this guy. At the end of his sermon, he gave an invitation for people to give their lives to Christ. Both of those boys went forward and became Christians.

One of them was a tall, skinny kid named Billy Graham. His best friend, Grady Wilson, accompanied him. The pair later launched the Billy Graham Evangelistic Association, through which Billy has spoken to more people about Jesus Christ than anybody in modern history. Grady Wilson served alongside Billy for fifty years, organizing the entire process.[2]

The world impact of those skinny teenagers was possible all because of one guy who almost no one has heard of. No, I'm not thinking of Mordecai Ham. I'm thinking of the usher who encouraged two disinterested teens to attend a church service. That usher had *skills*. God had gifted him to use those skills, and when he did, he changed history.

When you get a grip on the fact that you are called and gifted by God, it changes how you view yourself and frees you from insecurity and inferiority.

Reason #4—Discovering Your God-Given Gifts Helps Keep You Motivated and Encouraged

We are motivated and encouraged when we are doing what we're supposed to be doing, and we are not when we're not. There's a reason I'm not in accounting, architecture, art, or aviation, and that's only for starters, brought to you by the letter *A*. Nothing feels more draining than trying to do what God has *not* wired you to do. Life becomes a grind when you try to live apart from the gifts He's given you. When you are doing what God has wired you to do, you have energy.

"Ray, you have eight services every weekend and you speak at six of them," someone once said to me. "Aren't you exhausted?"

"No," I said, "I'm energized!" I would be far more exhausted after balancing a spreadsheet, examining patients, or counseling a frustrated person for an hour, than I am speaking six times over a weekend. I feel a little sorry for the people who come to my first message, because I'm far more fired up by the third or fourth. By the sixth service, it's, "Let's rock and *roll*!"

Using your God-given gifts is the best way to make a lasting impact. When I use the gifts God has given me, I feel energized to do what most positively affects others. Then, when I see what God does through those gifts, my internal fires get stoked all the more.

After I became a Christian, I had no idea that I might have speaking gifts. A tiny church in my hometown asked me to serve as a youth pastor, to reach a bunch of teenagers who were getting into a lot of trouble. They offered me two hundred dollars a month. I thought, *I'm rich!* But I told them, "Let me think and pray about it." I prayed for an opportunity to speak, because I knew that if I couldn't speak effectively, I'd have to lean on others to do a big part of my job.

A short while later, a friend named Cal invited me to speak on a Thursday night to about one hundred fifty kids at a junior high camp. I agreed. I prepped. I sweated. I had no idea if I would bomb. I got up front, and about three minutes after I started, these kids looked riveted. It shocked me. At the end of my talk, I gave an invitation to know Christ, and about half the kids in the room raised their hands. Then I totally forgot what to do next.

"Cal," I said, "come on up. I have no idea where to take them from here, but they're ready."

I walked away that night thinking, *I'm supposed to be doing this.* Then I thought, *I better learn how to do an altar call.*

Reason #5—Discovering Your God-Given Gifts Is the Best Way to Change the World

God says to you and to me, "I would like to do a great work in the world, and to accomplish that, I plan to use the gifts I placed inside you."

Some time ago we learned of a town in Cambodia where 100 percent of the girls, as young as four years old, were used in the sex traffic industry. A man who went to work there told us, "They have no other options." So the man decided to create some houses where the girls could live for free, develop some factories where they could work and earn a living, and build an alternative for them. He came to me one day and said, "We need help."

We responded by looking for a whole bunch of people in our church who were gifted with the ability to serve. We looked for another group with the gift of giving. Since then, God has used those gifts to build several good homes and support a factory—and the initiative has cut sex trafficking in that town by *50 percent*. That's the kind of thing God wants to do in our world through the gifts He has placed within all of us.

God wants to get to work *through* the gifts He has entrusted to you. If you see something in your community that needs fixing or improvement, could it be that God is leading you to get busy in exactly that place by using your gifts?

When men and women discover and use their God-given gifts, they get freed up to be themselves, which releases resources into the world. When you discover and use your gifts, you find yourself able to affirm others instead of chopping them down, which frees up yet more resources. And regularly using your gifts motivates you toward eager sacrifice, which frees up even more resources to do the work God wants to see accomplished in this world.

Life changing? You bet! World changing? Absolutely!

Reason #6—Discovering Your God-Given Gifts Frees You from Fear of Failure

"What if I try something and it doesn't work?" In that case, you've just discovered another thing for which you're not gifted. Don't beat yourself up over it. Just move on to the next thing. The list of things I'm not good at is twenty times longer than the list of things I am good at. Far from bothering me, that truth frees me in countless ways.

After I became a youth pastor, I got a guitar because I thought all youth pastors were supposed to play the guitar for group worship. It was a complete disaster. People came up to me afterward and said, "Are you okay?"

"Are you *kidding* me?" I said. "God does not want me doing *this*." I gave the guitar to a guy who could actually play it, and off he went.

Thomas Edison said, "I never failed once. It just happened to be [a] 2,000 step process."[3] Discovering our gifts is a multistep process for all of us. Your gifts are not going to be just like someone else's, so you have to dig for them. Please fail. Fast. It helps you find your gifts, plus it gives you funny stories to tell for the rest of your life.

Reason #7—Discovering Your God-Given Gifts Lowers Stress and Increases Joy

Life is a lot more fun when we use our God-given gifts.

As I write this I'm looking forward to the weekend. We have twelve thousand people descending on our church campus, and I have the incredible privilege of speaking to them. The second most common fear people have is public speaking, but I look forward to it. I'm not nervous; I'm excited. Now, if you told me I had to sing this weekend, I'd be stressed out (and so would the church). If you told me I had to run the technology for the service, I'd flip out. If you told me I had to find a parking spot for every car or an empty chair for every person, I'd check out. If you told me I had nursery duty, I'd pass out. If you told me I had to count the offering, balance it, and prepare it to meet the specifications of the church bookkeeper, I'd run out screaming.

It doesn't bother me that there are so many things I'm not good at, perhaps tasks that other pastors would have mastered by now. God has a whole army of gifted people. Each of us gets the privilege of doing what God has gifted, called, and wired us to do.

Why would anyone want to live any other way?

Four Steps to Find and Use Your Gifts

The greatest thing about discovering and developing your gifts is that it frees you to be yourself. God hasn't gifted anybody to do everything. When you find and use your gifts, you will be encouraged to trust God for what's next. What could be more encouraging? You can stop trying to be everybody else.

Here are four steps to get you started:

1. Decide

You will never possess what you are unwilling to pursue.

Decide that discovering your God-given gifts is worth pursuing. Take the time to get a grip on the gifts God has given you, and it will change the course and impact of your life. When the Bible says, "Each one has received a [spiritual] gift" (1 Peter 4:10 NKJV), that includes you, *even if it does not look like it.* It's clear in the Bible.

Evaluate how each of the gifts corresponds to your own experience. Ask believers who care for you what they think you're good at. Then *experiment* by trying out various tasks and jobs. Again, ask believers who care for you how you did. Believe me, they're dying to tell how your exuberant guitar playing works for *them.*

Some people say, "I'm waiting for God to tell me what He wants me to do with my life." That's too bad, because it's not going to happen. You can't steer a parked car. You have to be moving. If you're moving, God can steer you. Get out there and volunteer for something, anything. Just get moving. Could you be the Roof, Soffit, and Gutters Guy at the home-building project? The Soup Mama at the homeless shelter? The Clean-Up Kid at the bake sale? Try stuff. Use all the information you gather to discover how God has wired you.

God often gives supernatural gifts that match a person's natural gifts, but He also enjoys giving gifts that seem just the opposite. Years ago, a man named Kent Tucker played tight end for UCLA. Every year, the guys in his fraternity wanted to make him their president, and every year he turned them down because the required two-minute acceptance speech scared him to death. Public speaking totally intimidated him. Once he became a Christian, however, he discovered that God had (unfortunately, he thought) given him an influencing gift. He went to seminary and became an *incredible* communicator. In fact, he was the speaker at the camp where my wife became a Christian. He would still tell you, "It's the opposite of any natural talent I ever had."

2. Discover

Make a commitment to read and examine four major passages in the Bible that discuss God-given gifts: Romans 12:4–7; 1 Corinthians 12–14; Ephesians 4:11–13; and 1 Peter 4:8–11. Understand what those verses say. Think about how the various gifts work.

The following chart gives you a breakdown. People tend to be drawn to a specific area, and their gifts fall into one of the following five areas.

Categories of Spiritual Gifts

Guiding Gifts (Make Things Happen)	Pastor-Teacher, Apostleship, Leadership, Administration
Influencing Gifts (Communicate God's Word)	Evangelism, Teaching, Preaching (Prophecy)
Fellowship Gifts (Care for God's People)	Mercy, Pastoring, Hospitality, Healing, Encouragement, Exhortation
Task Gifts (Support God's Work)	Helps, Giving, Craftsmanship, Intercession
Support Gifts (Complement Other Gifts)	Wisdom, Knowledge, Discernment, Faith, Tongues, Miracles

3. Develop

You get good at something only through practice. You develop your gifts by using your gifts. The more you develop them, the better you get at using them, and the more fulfilled and effective you become. Keep exploring and using the gifts you discover.

4. Deploy

Take your gifts, plug them into service, and let God do whatever He wants to do through them. Do not approach your gifts with a preconceived notion of how God will use them. Never forget that *He* gifted you with them. Your job is to deploy them wherever He puts you.

Those four—*decide, discover, develop, deploy*—will lead you to some of the most exciting places imaginable. However, the spark to taking these four steps is the belief that God *has* gifted you, even when you aren't sure what those gifts are or whether they even exist.

Back in 1915, Ira Yates owned a dry-goods store in Rankin, Texas, that did about five thousand dollars' worth of business each month. A Pecos County rancher named Thomas Hickox noted the store's modest success and proposed that Yates trade the store for his 16,640-acre River Ranch, way out in northern Pecos County.

A friend who once owned the property warned Yates against the trade. He said, "Even buffalo know better than to cross the Pecos. A crow would not fly over it, and it is not worth the taxes."

Yates made the trade anyway. Years later, Yates's granddaughter explained that while her grandpa "didn't know beans about groceries," he did know ranching, and he wanted to get his hands on this large parcel of land.

For a very long decade, Ira and his wife, Ann, made a hardscrabble living off the desolate ranch. Desperate for a way to pay mounting debts, Ira approached the Transcontinental Oil Company in San Angelo about drilling some test wells on his property. Experts had declared no oil could be found west of the Pecos River, but on the off chance of finding something, the company drilled four wells.

On October 28, 1926, Yates became an instant millionaire. One of the wells produced a gusher that sent crude oil hundreds of feet into the air, just like in the movies. The first five wells together produced more than nine thousand barrels of crude a day, more than could be stored or moved. Oil production peaked in 1929, when the Yates Oil Field shipped out forty-one million barrels. The "worthless" ranch produced its one billionth barrel in 1985. Today, oil continues to flow from the Yates Oil Field, one of the largest reserves in the world.[4]

For more than a decade, Ira and Ann Yates labored to scratch out a meager existence, constantly worried about how to pay their bills—all because they had no idea what lay just under their feet. God says in essence, "I created you. I have put some priceless things deep inside you. Take the time to discover them and get them out, and they will make all the difference to your future, to those around you, to the world."

Until you look, you're usually not even aware that the gifts are there. The apostle Paul wrote, "Now about spiritual gifts, I don't want you to be unaware" (1 Corinthians 12:1, author's paraphrase). Once you are aware of it, he added, "Do not neglect your gift" (1 Timothy 4:14).

The Gifts/Joy Connection

The words *joy* and *gifts* and *grace* are all the same word in the original Bible Greek—*charis*. (Something else from seminary!) This factoid tells me that when we use our gifts, we build joy and grace into our lives.

The best feeling in the world comes from using our gifts for God's purposes. The biggest thrill in the universe is to be used by God for something He wants to accomplish. I love sports, but the greatest excitement any of us will ever know is when we get in the game and use our gifts to team up with God to do something remarkable in the world.

God created you for service. He called you to service. He will reward you for service. You are indispensable to service. Chuck Swindoll put it this way:

> Nobody is a whole team. Each one is a player. But take away one player and the game is forfeited.
>
> Nobody is a whole orchestra. Each one is a musician. But take away one musician and the symphony is incomplete. . . .
>
> None of us is a whole, independent, self-sufficient, supercapable, all-powerful hot-shot, let's quit acting like we are. Life's lonely enough without our playing that silly role.[5]

We need each other if we are to find hope. You need someone and someone needs you.

We will talk more about working together in the next chapter. Just think for now, what "Yates Oil Field" is just waiting to be unleashed in your own life?

A Brit named Jack Harris lost his elderly wife and took up jigsaw puzzles to occupy his mind. Over time, he chose more and more complex puzzles. He finally tackled a five-thousand-piece puzzle depicting a 150-year-old painting of the return of the prodigal son. He worked on the puzzle for hours each day for more than seven years. When he was eighty-six years old, he was finally ready to finish the puzzle—4,999 pieces already in place—and he couldn't find piece number 5,000. The only thing he could imagine was that somehow that piece had fallen off the table and the dog ate it. Jack was distraught. The puzzle was no longer being manufactured. But when the company that created the puzzle heard about his problem, they crafted a one-of-a-kind piece, and Jack finished the job.[6]

Almost everybody I know could sympathize with that. Who hasn't put together a puzzle and discovered the last piece is missing? The problem is, when every puzzle piece is in place *except* for one, what is the only thing you notice when you look at that puzzle? The missing piece. That's a God's-eye view when you're not functioning using your gifts.

Perhaps you believe that no one will miss you if you drop off the table somehow. Nothing could be further from the truth. God's perspective is, "I have a one-of-a-kind spot, just for you." God created you as a unique individual, and without you, the puzzle remains unfinished.

There are people, churches, and causes that will never reach their God-given potential if you don't find your God-given gifts and step into place. Surprising as it may seem to you, you may be the exact missing puzzle piece some group, some person, some church is looking for right now as you read this.

9.

FIVE: REFUSE TO GO IT ALONE

Two are better than one because they have a good return for their labor. For if either of them falls, the one will lift up his companion. But woe to the one who falls when there is not another to lift him up.

ECCLESIASTES 4:9–10 NASB

Walking with a friend in the dark is better than walking alone in the light.

HELEN KELLER

The success or failure of your life is largely determined by the equipment you use. You wouldn't try to fight a forest fire with a squirt gun. You wouldn't try to fly across the Pacific Ocean with a hang glider. You wouldn't try to hit a baseball without a bat. You have to use the right equipment. Fortunately, God has provided the equipment you need to make it in life. The most overlooked essential equipment needed is connected relationships. I'm going to lay out for you five relationships we all need. Before I do, let me tell you why this matters.

Two decades ago, I sat mesmerized in the ballroom of the Hyatt Hotel and Convention Center in Chicago listening to the world's leading expert on stress. She said, "All of us have stress. Anyone who wants to get rid of stress doesn't understand it. A stress-free life is not an option. Not having stress means you're dead. However, there is good stress and bad stress. Healthy stress and destructive stress."

The expert explained that healthy stress requires we have three elements in equal balance. Those key elements are control, challenge, and support.

"How people put these three things together will determine whether they will be ascending or in decline in every relationship they have," the expert said.

Everyone needs *controls*. Without financial controls, schedule controls, discipline, or focus, we end up stressed and in trouble. (If you don't believe that adequate controls are needed, just ask any Bernie Madoff investor.)

Second, *challenges* are essential. Anybody who isn't being challenged or stretched is probably deteriorating.

In 1982, two Soviet cosmonauts broke a record by spending 211 days in space. Television cameras prepared for the two guys to return. A band waited to wave flags and lead the triumphant parade celebrating the accomplishment of communism.

The door opened. The band played. The people cheered. The television cameras zoomed in. And nothing happened. Weak from months of inactivity, the cosmonauts were unable to stand up. Zero-gravity living had deteriorated their muscles to the point where they had to be carried from their seats. They broke endurance records but could not stand or walk for months because their hearts were no longer strong enough to pump blood even twelve inches to their brains. In response, the Soviets invented a "penguin suit," which is basically an athletic suit laced with rubber bands that causes constant resistance. By wearing a penguin suit, muscles continue to develop and are spared from atrophy.[1]

Let me admit this: I long for a zero-gravity life with no problems, no resistance, no challenges, and no stress, but God knows better. He knows that we need some resistance and some challenges, because the easier our lives are, the weaker our spiritual muscles will become.

The third component that forms the foundation for controls and challenges is *support*. Support is so crucial to the equation that the expert spent the majority of the next hour talking about how to build a base of support. That hour was a game changer for me.

If you're like me, you are probably making an instant assessment to see if these three areas are in balance in your life. And if you're like me, you are probably discovering that your number one need is for support. Most people have enough control with jobs, taxes, family, and the government. Most people have enough challenges to last for the next thousand years. Between life, marriage, kids, finances, ministry, health, and Washington, DC, I have enough controls *and* challenges. Probably so do you.

Most people have far more challenges than they need and way more controls than they want. Our lifelong battle is to develop adequate amounts of support to stay encouraged in life and in leadership. With enough support, the challenges, problems, and roadblocks that come our way don't bother us as much. To achieve this, we have to answer a central question: "How do I build enough support in my life to face challenges with energy?" Getting right down to it, let's just ask, "Am I close to anyone?"

In the mid-1960s, the last of the team of brothers who founded the Warner Brothers film empire sold all of his stock for $32 million, the equivalent of roughly $250 million today. After the sale, Jack Warner was sad when no one showed up for his tennis parties anymore. A friend said, "Jack, you're so alone in this world." Jack replied, "If you have power, you can't have friends."

Jack spent more than four decades in an iron-fisted career that earned him a reputation for both brilliant success and jaw-dropping ruthlessness. He once maneuvered in secret to oust his brothers from control of their own company. Harry never spoke to Jack again.

Jack was unfaithful in each of his marriages. Yet when his son from his first wife criticized the new wife Jack was cheating on, Jack never spoke to his son again. He not only renounced him but even wrote him out of his autobiography. At his funeral, so few people attended that the rabbi moved the service from the temple to a small chapel upstairs.[2] Jack Warner was a great example of a man who died rich yet in abject poverty. So why is it that millions in our day continue to follow in Jack's lonely footsteps? Is it possible we really don't understand that hope inevitably fades without supportive relationships to help it thrive?

Friendships That Give Support

In Robert Putnam's influential analysis of social relationships, *Bowling Alone: The Collapse and Revival of American Community*, he wrote, "The single most common finding from a half century's research on the correlates of life satisfaction, not only in the United States but around the world, is that happiness is best predicted by the breadth and depth of one's social connections."[3]

The best example for Putnam's research might be Winston Churchill, the celebrated prime minister of Great Britain during World War II. Churchill connected deeply with all kinds of people throughout his life. He had a strong marriage, solid family relationships, a lot of close friends, and a large number of successful relationships at work. On the other hand, he had terrible health habits. He smoked cigars all the time, drank too much, had an unhealthy diet, had bizarre sleep habits, and never worked out. Yet he lived to be ninety years old.

When his doctor once asked him whether he ever exercised, Churchill replied, "I get all the exercise I need being a pallbearer for all my friends who run and do exercises."[4]

Churchill no doubt would have approved of another statement from

Bowling Alone: "As a rough rule of thumb, if you belong to no groups, but you decide to join one, you've cut your risk of dying in the next year in half."[5]

At Bayside, we came up with a catchy motto for our small groups ministry: "Join a Group or Die."

In the Bible, godly people routinely sought the support of others. One of my favorite lines in all the Old Testament says, "Jonathan, Saul's son, rose and went to David at Horesh, and strengthened his hand in God" (1 Samuel 23:16 ESV). Can you imagine how David's hope soared in the middle of extraordinarily difficult circumstances when his friend went out of his way to seek him out and encourage him? The story calls all of us to ask a critical question: Do I have someone in my life who "strengthens my hand in God"? We all need one, or more, and fast!

The Best Investment You'll Ever Make

Meaningful friendships increase your life span and benefit your health, your marriage, and your ability on the job. Never underestimate the power of close friends. Rabbi Harold Kushner tells a great story about the amazing power of connection:

> I was sitting on a beach one summer day, watching two children, a boy and a girl, playing in the sand. They were hard at work building an elaborate sand castle by the water's edge, with gates and towers and moats and internal passages. Just when they had nearly finished their project, a big wave came along and knocked it down, reducing it to a heap of wet sand. I expected the children to burst into tears, devastated by what had happened to all their hard work. But they surprised me. Instead, they ran up the shore away from the water, laughing and holding hands, and sat down to build another castle. I realized that they had taught me an important lesson. All the things in our lives, all the complicated structures we spend so much time and energy creating, are built on sand. Sooner or later, the wave will come along and knock down what we have worked so hard to build up. When that happens, only the person who has somebody's hand to hold will be able to laugh.[6]

Friendship is the best investment you'll ever make. Without close friendships, your Hope Quotient plunges—which will make it nearly impossible for you to reach your potential.

A Fortune 500 CEO stopped at a gas station while his wife went inside to pay for the gas. He watched as she had an animated but pleasant conversation with the man working inside. When she returned to the car, her curious husband asked, "Who were you talking to?"

"He was an old boyfriend," she said. "Isn't that unbelievable?"

Her husband smiled and said, "Man, I'll bet you're glad you married me—a Fortune 500 CEO instead of a service station attendant."

She paused, then replied, "No, that's not what I was thinking at all. I was thinking, *You're fortunate that I married you, or he'd be the Fortune 500 CEO and you'd be the gas station attendant*."[7] With solid, supportive relationships in place, you can go far!

Years ago, when my son Scott was ten years old, the two of us decided to try out a trampoline I'd just bought.

"Be careful!" my wife said. We were, until the moment she left. Then we soon discovered, like everyone else who owns a trampoline, that if you synchronize your jumps, you both can go much higher.

At one point, we timed our jumps perfectly. Scott took off like a rocket and I watched as he soared above me, airborne. Moments later, he crashed back down to the trampoline and we both laughed our heads off—not realizing that Mom had come back and was standing there, glaring. By then we had already proven the point that you can go a lot higher by doing life with somebody else.

Friendships lift you because they provide encouragement, support during tough times, and healthy accountability. "He who walks with the wise grows wise, but a companion of fools suffers harm" (Proverbs 13:20).

The brilliant psychologist Larry Crabb wrote, "The core battle in everyone's life is to relate well to God, to worship him, enjoy him, experience his presence, hear his voice, trust him in everything, always call him good, obey every command (even the hard ones), and hope in him when he seems to disappear."[8]

Crabb concluded, "That's the battle the community of God is called to enter in each other's lives."[9] *That's a battle I cannot win alone.* I need a community that is waging the same war to include me in the fight.

None of us can win the battle alone, and God didn't design us to win alone. We win the lifelong battle to stay encouraged and hold on to hope only as we join others who need our help to win their battles as well.

A local Christian hero and statesman, Bryce Jessup, said the key to his whole life and his stellar twenty-five-year run as a college president boils down to one line: "Dream a dream and build a team."[10]

I'd add only that a dream without a team is merely a wish. Who is on *your* team?

The Five Relationships We All Need

Every one of us needs at least five types of key relationships. Our friends and colleagues are not created equal. Different kinds of relationships help us in various ways. Surprisingly, not all of these relationships need to be in person. Sometimes, these relationships can come through books. As Charlie "Tremendous" Jones says, "You are the same today as you'll be in five years except for two things, the books you read and the people you meet."[11] We need all the help we can get.

1. Vision Casters

Ralph Waldo Emerson wrote, "Our chief want in life is, somebody who shall make us do what we can."[12] I really like this statement, enough to create my own version: what we all need is someone who will give us a vision for who we can be, far beyond anything we ever imagined.

I need people who stretch my vision and help me dream bigger dreams. I want individuals around me who have a way of sparking huge new vision. Just this morning, I read a sermon transcript from Seattle pastor Mark Driscoll and he became a new Vision Caster to me. He helped me think about a new way to do a piece of ministry, and we're already planning how that fresh vision could become a major catalyst for new growth.

My friend Glen Cole, who believed in the impossible, did the same thing for me when I got to his home turf of Sacramento to start a new church. He didn't view me as competition but as someone to help bring in the harvest. He helped me consider new initiatives, imagine what could be, and see things that had been invisible. What would my life and ministry have been without Glen's influence?

Henrietta Mears died fifty years ago, but she is still a Vision Caster for me. She worked for years as the Christian education director at Hollywood Presbyterian Church and is perhaps most remembered for her 1953 book, *What the Bible Is All About*.[13] That multimillion seller is still so popular they printed a revised edition in 2011. How many sixty-year-old books do you know of that have enough juice in them to warrant a revision? Henrietta also founded the Gospel Light Publishing Company and Gospel Literature International, as well as the Forest Home Christian conference center in Southern California. She significantly influenced world-class leaders such as Billy Graham, Campus Crusade founder Bill Bright, former Senate chaplain Richard Halverson, and Young Life founder Jim Rayburn, among other leading lights. Her auto-biography of a remarkable life is appropriately titled *Dream Big: The Henrietta Mears Story*.[14]

Henrietta Mears's most inspiring quote is, "There is no magic in small plans. When I consider my ministry, I think of the world. Anything less than that would not be worthy of Christ nor of His will for my life."[15] Wow! *That's* vision!

2. Soul Sharpeners

Here is the Soul Sharpener's job description: "As iron sharpens iron, so one man sharpens another" (Proverbs 27:17).

Some people turn you on spiritually and some people turn you off spiritually. Hang around with those who turn you on. A Soul Sharpener helps you develop spiritually, daring you to be all you can be in the spiritual arena. He or she will not let you settle for second best.

A long time ago, a wise man told me, "The best way to grow is to be the smallest person in the room."

During my youth pastor days, I got a call one afternoon from Youth Specialties, the largest Christian youth organization on the planet. They called to ask if I would consider joining the speaking team. Now, the founders of Youth Specialties, Wayne Rice and Mike Yaconelli, were the big shots in that arena and between them had published something like a hundred books, in addition to running massive conferences. The YS team already had six other guys just like them.

The first time I walked into a room packed with these dudes, I thought, *This room is filled with famous speakers, world-class leaders, prolific writers . . . and then there's me.* It was like the children's picture game, "Find the one that doesn't fit." *I don't belong here*, I thought. *These guys are all better than me.* I found a friend and confided how intimidated, insignificant, and out of place I felt there. He said with bursting excitement the exact opposite of what I expected to hear.

"This is *perfect!*" he said. "The best way to grow as a communicator is to be the worst communicator in the room. *That's you!* The best way to grow as a writer is to be the worst writer in the room. *That's you!* [Does it show?] And the best way to grow as a leader is to be the smallest leader in the room. *You again!*"

His words reframed the way I saw my place at Youth Specialties. I spent ten great years with the organization, which remains the single best thing that ever happened to me as a communicator. Those leaders all became Soul Sharpeners for me. Just being on the team stepped up my game in those areas.

The experience also taught me this massive lesson: if we let insecurities drive us away from tough circumstances, we will never grow.

3. Models and Mentors

"People seldom improve when they have no model but themselves to copy after," said the poet Oliver Goldsmith.[16] The apostle Paul wrote to young Christians, "Follow my example, as I follow the example of Christ" (1 Corinthians 11:1). Paul told a more seasoned group of believers, "Whatever you have learned or received or heard from me, or seen in me—put it into practice" (Philippians 4:9). I wonder if the Christian leader Oswald Chambers had any of this in mind when he wrote, "The way we grow in holiness is to be around people more holy than ourselves."[17] (I don't know about you, but in my case, that's pretty easy to find!)

I like to have between three and six models and mentors at all times. They have enriched every area of my life.

Growing up in a broken, alcoholic home, I knew I had seen a pattern that I did not want to repeat. I will be forever grateful for Peter and Carol Schreck, both PhDs in marriage and family counseling. We were neighbors in Southern California for five years, and Peter pastored the church in Southern California I attended. Between dinners, tennis matches, and observing their family, I began to think for the first time that I could actually have a thriving marriage. I learned from them what a marriage looked like, what commitment looked like, what parenting looked like, and what a family looked like. They also taught me the invaluable place of mentors and models.

4. Heart Healers

Dr. Paul Tournier wrote, "It is impossible to overemphasize the immense need men have to be really listened to, to be taken seriously, to be understood. . . . No one can develop freely in this world and find a full life without feeling understood by at least one person."[18]

At one critical point in his friendship with David, Jonathan asked his dear friend to "reaffirm his oath out of love for him, because he loved him as he loved himself" (1 Samuel 20:17). Jonathan and David served as Heart Healers for each other.

The condition of our hearts is one of life's determining factors. There will be times when we all suffer from hearts that are broken or cynical or hard or discouraged. We all have times of despair. People of hope suffer these things, just as others do. But people of hope also work to bring Heart Healers into their circle of friends, because they know they will be in better emotional shape because of them.

5. Tail Kickers

Tail Kickers love us enough to tell us the truth. "Wounds from a friend can be trusted, but an enemy multiplies kisses" (Proverbs 27:6). You recognize tail-kicking kinds of people by the gigantic boot mark they leave on the seat of your pants.

You will not always like what a Tail Kicker has to say. A Tail Kicker is who Oscar Wilde described when he wrote, "True friends stab you in the front."[19]

Former United States secretary of state Henry Kissinger was a Tail Kicker of legendary proportions. His speechwriter, Winston Lord, prepared many difficult speeches on complicated topics. Lord recalls taking a draft of a speech to him, and Kissinger rebuffing him with, "Is this the best you can do?" Lord reworked the speech many times, only to be met with the same gruff comment each time. On the ninth draft, Lord said to Kissinger, "I've beaten my brains out. I know it's the best I can do. I can't possibly improve one more word." Kissinger looked at him and said, "In that case, now I'll read it."[20]

If the task of some people is to comfort the afflicted, then the task of Tail Kickers is to afflict the comfortable. God uses Tail Kickers to move us forward, to stay faithful, and to make us get after it. They challenge us to stop settling. They remind us to keep getting back up.

One of my best friends has this gift. Last year, our ministry faced several challenges at the same time. I called him expecting sympathy (dumb move). He listened, then he restored my perspective and confidence with one statement. He said, "Ray, I want to ask you one question: How would a great leader handle this?" It was just what I needed.

True Friends Are True Wealth

Sometimes it seems the *only* thing that can get your hopes up after they've been dashed is a friend. The story is told of a high school student who wasn't feeling well. After a few doctor visits, the doctor delivered devastating news.

"I'm sorry, son, but you have cancer. That's the bad news. The good news is, it is operable. Your long-term prognosis is excellent, but you'll need surgery, radiation, and chemotherapy. That process will make you lose all your hair."

The young man checked out of school, went through surgery, and completed six weeks of chemotherapy. All of his hair was gone the day he went to the doctor and got a clean bill of health. The doctor cleared him to start back to school the very next day.

The whole way home, the teen was quiet. His mom said, "Honey, you ought be excited about this. You get to go back to school, see your friends."

"Mama, I'm bald," he said. "They'll make fun of me."

"What if we get you a toupee?"

"Mom, that would make it worse. They'd snatch it off my head and throw it around."

"What about a hat?"

"Mom!"

It's not hard to picture the kid's dejection. He got more depressed the farther they drove from the doctor's, because the next day he was going to have to wake up and, for the first time, his *very* worst fears were going to come true. He was going to be a fifteen-year-old walking onto a high school campus *very* bald. He knew he'd be made fun of by every student at the school.

"I wonder if I should just take the rest of the year off and have them send me homework," he said. "I don't want to see anybody. I don't want to see my friends. I don't want to spend the rest of the year embarrassed."

The mom pulled into the driveway. They walked together into the dark house and she turned on the light. Seventy people screamed, *"Surprise!"*

Seventy of his friends from school were in his living room—and every guy had shaved his head.

There is power, encouragement, and freedom from anxiety in friendship. Things just go better when you don't do life alone. Build a base of support. Not only will you *be* better, but you'll *feel* better.

One final note. Friendships are not found—they're built. Working with people for thirty years, I've talked to *so many* people who say they can't find friends. There is no "tree of friends" somewhere that you need to find. Today would be a great day to start doing *something* to build some friendships. You, and they, will be glad you did.

10.

SIX: REPLACE BURNOUT WITH BALANCE

You chart the path ahead of me and tell me where to stop and rest.

PSALM 139:3 NLT

Christ is risen; I'm dead.

RAY JOHNSTON, AFTER

FOURTEEN EASTER SERVICES

Years ago, I was hired to do leadership development for an organization of about a thousand churches. My first responsibility was to put on a national leadership conference. In February. In Chicago. At least people would attend the meetings because nobody would want to be outside. As expected, the room was packed. For the first session, I introduced Jim Burns. I figured Jim was an outstanding choice—a twenty-year veteran of working with parents of teenagers, president of HomeWord Ministries, and author of forty books.

I sat down feeling pretty good about how the conference was going, which was a good thing because as I scanned the room, I realized that every big shot in the whole organization was in it. I had a sudden thought that every one of them was staring at me and thinking, *We spent some real money to make this conference happen, so this had better be good.*

Then I thought, *Burns had better be* great.

Jim began his message by saying, "Fifteen years ago, when I first got into ministry and leadership . . . I had an affair."

I sank in my chair. *I am so fired.*

Jim paused, and then added, "But it was not with another woman."

I sank even lower. *I'm fired today.*

Jim continued, "It also wasn't with a man. Fifteen years ago, I had an affair, and it almost destroyed my marriage. I had an affair and I almost lost my kids. I had an affair and I almost lost my ministry. I had an affair and it almost wrecked my health. I had an affair—with my career."

I straightened up and thought, *Jim, this is awesome. You just saved my job!*

"All my extra time went to my career. All my extra energy went to my career. All my extra emotions went to my career. My career was all I thought about, and I almost lost my family and my ministry."

Then in an unforgettable moment, Jim delivered one of those great statements you never forget. He said, "If the devil can't make you bad, he'll just make you busy, because it will have the same effect."

Then I thought, *Jim, you just might have saved a whole lot of people's jobs* and *marriages.*

Strangled by Stress

When we are overloaded, overcommitted, we lose. We lose joy, we lose confidence, we lose peace, we lose friendships, we endure life instead of enjoy life, we are grouchy, irritable, discouraged. We sacrifice family closeness, we end up less productive, and worst of all, we end up out of touch with God and everybody in our lives. In other words, we lose hope.

Dr. Richard Swenson would say we are out of "margin," the title of his best-selling book.[1] Margin is the space between your load and your limit. Most of us are loaded far beyond our limits. That means we have no margin in our lives. Swenson wrote:

The conditions of modern day living devour margin . . .

Marginless is being thirty minutes late to the doctor's office because you were twenty minutes late getting out of the hairdresser, because you were ten minutes late dropping the children off at school, because the car ran out of gas two blocks from the gas station, and you forgot your purse. That's marginless.

Margin, on the other hand, is having breath at the top of the staircase, money at the end of the month, and sanity left over after adolescence.

Marginless is the baby crying and the phone ringing at the same time. Margin is Grandma taking care of the baby for the afternoon.

Marginless is being asked to carry a load five pounds heavier than you can lift. Margin is having a friend to help carry half the burden.

Marginless is not having enough time to finish the book you're reading on stress (don't stop, keep going). Margin is having the time to read it twice.

Marginless is fatigue. Margin is energy.

Marginless is red ink. Margin is black ink.

Marginless is hurry. Margin is calm.

Marginless is our culture. Margin is counter-culture, having some space and life in your schedule.

Marginless is reality. Margin is remedy.

Marginless is the disease (of our decade).

Margin is the cure.[2]

The challenge of balancing our lives is getting worse—for you—for me—for everybody.

- Seventy-five to ninety percent of all doctor office visits are for stress-related ailments and complaints.[3]
- The most-stressed employees develop heart problems at a 79 percent higher rate than their less-stressed peers.[4]
- Stress is the most common cause of long-term sickness absence for employees.[5]
- Forty-three percent of Americans between the ages of thirteen

and sixty-four say they rarely or never get a good night's sleep on weeknights.[6]

- About two-thirds (63 percent) of Americans say their sleep needs are not being met during the week.[7]

More than at any time in history, we are chronically rushed, habitually late, regularly exhausted, continually pressured, desperately overloaded, totally overwhelmed, and vastly overcommitted. Do you know even one overcommitted, frantic, rushed, hurried, stressed-out person who enjoys high levels of hope? I don't either. We ought to have warning labels affixed to our foreheads: "Warning! Contents under pressure! Extreme danger of explosion!"

Two years ago, a thought hit me that resonated not only with me but with a group of pastors who were complaining about burnout. I had one of the major *aha!* moments of my life with them. "Could I make an observation?" I said after listening for a while, and even chiming in myself. "I think we're all acting like we're burned out, but we're actually all discouraged."

The room got quiet for a moment, and then everybody agreed. "Yep, that's it."

I've now come to believe that discouragement *often* masks itself as burnout. As pastors, although we all said we felt burned out, in fact we were no busier than we had been two years earlier. I now recognize that when someone comes to me complaining, "I'm fried," very often discouragement lies at the root of the problem.

Discouragement often masquerades as burnout, and unchecked discouragement will kill hope.

Let me give you seven questions to ask yourself that may help bring things back into balance and lift your Hope Quotient.

Question #1—Is My Pace of Life Out of Control? (Because Anything Out of Control Is Headed for a Wreck)

If I want peace of mind, if I want better health, if I want better relationships, if I want to be more productive, if I want less stress, if I want more joy, if I am sick and tired of being sick and tired, then I have to pace myself. Take this Pace of Life Index to check yourself out:

Pace of Life Index

Score: Always or Usually (5)   Sometimes (3)   Seldom or Never (1)

---

1. Do you tend to fill every minute then strain
   to get it all done?   _____
2. Do you hate to be kept waiting?   _____
3. Do you drive, talk, and eat faster than other
   people around you?   _____
4. Do you multitask so much that you miss details?   _____
5. Do your spouse or children have to say your
   name repeatedly before you hear them?   _____
6. Do you forget what you ate the day before?   _____
7. Do you have to ask people to repeat themselves
   because your mind wanders?   _____
8. Do you become impatient with clerks and service people?   _____
9. Do you find it hard to unwind and relax?   _____
10. Do you clench your jaw or get migraine headaches?   _____

Total Score   _____

Scoring: 40–50*—High hurry sickness
           30–39—Medium hurry sickness
           20–29—Low hurry sickness

*Quick note to Type As: A perfect score of 50 doesn't mean you win.

Question #2—Am I Running on Empty?
(Because It's Hard to Fake "Full")

I love to jet ski. A while ago, in the middle of a lake with two guys on the back of my jet ski, a beeper went off. It warned me, "You're low on gas." I knew that if I didn't stop and refuel, we would soon find ourselves stranded and swimming.

That warning light got me thinking, *Wouldn't it be nice if God would warn me when I'm reaching my limit?* Imagine if God put a red flashing light right in your brain, or if a beeper went off on your forehead when you hit 110 percent capacity and an airport announcer voice said, "Warning! You're about to go on overload! Back off!"

God *has* given us a warning light on the dashboards of our lives. It's called loss of joy. When we're joyless, we're on overload. Having no joy means we are about to exceed a limit, whether physical, mental, spiritual, or emotional, and put ourselves in danger of shutting down and getting stranded in a place we never wanted to be.

I'm glad for a warning, because I'm so mission-driven and focused that, if I could, I would work eight days a week, twenty-six hours a day. If I head in that direction long enough, I start enduring life and using people instead of enjoying life and loving people.

For me it's pretty easy. I have a painful yet foolproof test. Once a year I ask my wife, "Am I more fun to live with than I was a year ago, or have I become more uptight?" For obvious reasons I conduct the test only *once* a year.

Here's another test, developed by Nancy Beach, that may be less painful. Check it out.

Your Spiritual Vital Signs[8]

Conduct your own heart check.

Rate yourself in five areas to test your spiritual health:

Emotions—Have you cried lately? Or really laughed? A healthy heart is fully aware of deep emotion—and can name it.

Moments—Are you present or preoccupied? Ask your spouse, children, or friends if you're "all there" when you're with them. They can say whether you're "skimming" key relationships.

Fun—Do you set aside time for enjoyment, whether active sports, quiet reading, arts, or crafts? When was the last time you really had fun?

People—Do you resent phone calls and people seeking you out? Or do you see them as opportunities for ministry? If you're running for cover, trying to dodge people, you're overextended.

Whispers—How long has it been since you heard the still, small voice? One of the first signs of a hardening heart is a deafened ear to the quiet promptings of God.

God wants you emotionally, spiritually, and relationally healthy. The apostle Paul described the kingdom of God as a matter of "righteousness, peace and joy in the Holy Spirit" (Romans 14:17). Of those three, righteousness can be faked, peace can be imitated, but joy is pretty hard to mimic, which makes it the best indicator of the true state of a soul. There's a glow to true joy that joking and silliness and horseplay just can't reproduce. When that glow fades, the warning light comes on.

None of us can afford to ignore the critical need to refuel. Here's a lifetime lifestyle tip: schedule times to recharge, refresh, and refuel in advance. Easter is busy for pastors. On Monday morning after Easter, I usually say, "Christ is risen; I'm dead." Since it *is* predictable, Carol and I will take a short vacation with some good friends about three or four weeks before the rush hits. We also block out a few days after Easter for a staff getaway to chill, golf, relax, and have fun. Planned refueling stops help to keep my joy level full and my hope level high.

Question #3—Am I Dropping the Right Balls?
(Because Some Balls Don't Bounce Back)

Several years ago in a university commencement address, Brian Dyson, CEO of Coca-Cola Enterprises, spoke on keeping life balanced. He said,

> Imagine life as a game in which you are juggling five balls in the air. You name them—work, family, health, friends, and spirit—and you're keeping all of these in the air. You will soon understand that work is a rubber ball. If you drop it, it will bounce back. But the other four balls—family, health, friends, and spirit—are made of glass. If you drop one of these, they will be irrevocably scuffed, marked, nicked, damaged, or even shattered. They will never be the same.[9]

Brilliant! A glass ball is not only more *fragile* than a rubber ball, but it's also more *valuable*.

Keep your priorities straight. Taking care of your spiritual life, your health, your relationships, and your spirit is not a selfish act. It's a sustaining one.

To juggle well, everyone has to learn to say no. It's a tough lesson for people pleasers. Saying yes to one means saying no to another. A guy in ministry once told me, "Every time somebody asks me to add something to my work schedule, I ask myself, 'Do I want to rob that time from my family to do it?'"

Relationships are like the fragile glass balls. Nothing takes the place of relationships. Fame doesn't. Wealth can't. Success won't.

Maybe you've seen a demonstration where the speaker puts a glass container on the stage with some big and small rocks next to it. A volunteer will try to put all the rocks in the jar, starting with the smallest rocks. When the volunteer starts with the small rocks, not all the big rocks will fit. But when the volunteer is told to put in the big rocks first, everything fits. The point is, start with the big rocks, the most important items, and the little rocks like the petty tasks and errands will find their place.

Relationships are like the huge rocks.

A friend just lost his elderly father. Right after his dad's death, my friend started converting old family slides into electronic files. He bought a machine and watched with keen interest as, slide by slide, images of his family's history went by. He converted more than five hundred slides, but he hardly glanced at most. Pictures flashed by of parades and cars and landscapes and fun trips to the zoo with his dad. Then he'd stop to stare awhile, because there before him were the images of people—boys and girls and men and women he knew and loved, and the dad his heart ached over. Giraffes are fun to see at the zoo, but fifty years later, it's the father gazing at the animal that captures a son's full attention.

It's paying attention to the most important stuff now that creates the unfading images later.

Question #4—Have I Stopped Believing I'm Invincible? (Because There Is a God, and I'm Not Him)

We all have limits. None of us can keep cramming our lives with more and more. God is infinite. We are anything but. "I have learned that everything has limits," wrote the psalmist (Psalm 119:96 GNT).

We tend to overestimate our abilities and underestimate our problems and how much time it will take to solve them. The culture insists we can do it all, have it all, be it all. It's a lie. Eve fell for it. We don't have to. We can't be like God and become whatever we want to be. We have limits. I can't sing like Michael Bublé or swim like Michael Phelps, and I doubt that you can either.

- *We have physical limits.* None of us can go a month without sleep (although some try!).
- *We have emotional limits.* None of us can cope with the weight of the whole world.
- *We have mental limits.* None of us can process all the information around us.
- *We have space limits.* None of us can be in more than one place at one time.

- *We have time limits.* None of us can cram more than twenty-four hours in a day, no matter how many time management books we read.

Moses kept it simple. "Know that the LORD is God; there is no other besides him" (Deuteronomy 4:35 ESV). Getting realistic about our limits will free us from overcommitment. That will restore energy, which leads to rising hope.

Question #5—When I Relax, Do I Feel Guilty? (Because Rest Is Not a Four-Letter Word)

A lot of life is like surfing. There are seasons when waves of opportunity come in and you just have to catch them while the surf's up. But then you have to ensure you take equal time off when the ocean is flat.

I want the people I work with to be happy and healthy. So to make sure our team actually has a life, we train our staff to do three things:

1. Divert daily.
2. Withdraw weekly.
3. Abandon annually.

Divert daily means to divide each day into three sections—morning to noon, noon to five, five and beyond. Most days, they don't work all three. Sounds simple, but when put into practice, it changes everything. A church has almost round-the-clock activities, with businesses that can be called only during the day and members who can be called or attend classes or rehearsals only at night. *Divert daily* helps team members balance it.

Withdraw weekly means to carve out one day a week for rest and focus on enjoying God. One day a lady called her pastor, very upset.

"I called all day Monday," she said, "and I couldn't get through to you."

"Monday is my day off," he said.

"Well, the *devil* never takes a day off!"

The pastor paused, then said, "When he becomes my model, I'll let you know."[10]

Abandon annually means getting away for an extended period from *all* the demands of work.

For people in high-pressure jobs, my experience says that one week of vacation does only some good. It takes one full week just to start to unwind. At about two weeks, they can finally start to relax.

When I tell people, "You have to take some time off," they often reply, "Ray, clearly you don't understand my life."

"I understand that *sometimes* you're too busy to check out for a while," is my standard response, "so you catch the waves when you have to. But make a point to catch them only when they come. Then take equal time off."

Carol and I look at the year ahead and can forecast certain waves. Recently, we went to Lake Tahoe alone together and said, "Ten years from now, what are we going to regret that we didn't do? Let's plan and book it *now*, before we lose the time forever. Let's dream up a couple of things and put them on the calendar, things that we would never do if we don't plan it and arrange for it right now."

We studied the decade ahead. Because we know that between now and then, surf's up.

Question #6—Do I Understand That God Makes a Big Deal of This? (Because This Really Is the Fourth Commandment)

The least obeyed verse in the Bible, in my opinion, is Psalm 46:10: "Be still, and know that I am God." However you picture getting the rest you need—surfing, balancing, or something else—don't forget that God makes a huge deal of it, enough to inscribe "Keep the Sabbath" on a stone tablet.

These three things *have* to happen:

• Resting physically. During the French Revolution the nation outlawed the "Sabbath" because they wanted people to work. A few years later they had to reinstate it because the health of the nation had collapsed.[11]

- Refocusing spiritually. Watching a ball game won't give you a new perspective on life, but getting in touch with God will.
- Recharging emotionally. Solitude and being with people you love will recharge you. This represents the kind of e-mails I received in my office the last time I taught on burnout:

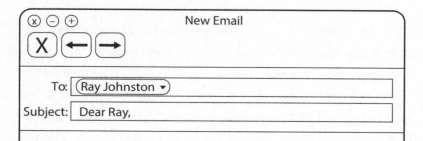

New Email

To: Ray Johnston ▾

Subject: Dear Ray,

Dear Ray,

I've been filling my life with activities, family, friends, and work. I think I had an unspoken goal to stay too busy to think about the issues I need to face. I finally rested yesterday. And the world did not come to an end. I started reading a book and wrote two long-overdue thank-yous. I didn't rush. Anywhere. I listened to my kids. Really listened. I looked hard at my house and realized how much I liked the decorating I'd done that I never found time to enjoy. I prayed. I thanked God for all His blessings—for everything around me that I stayed too busy even to notice. I asked Him what I was so afraid of, what kept me from sitting with Him. He didn't answer immediately, but I didn't really need it right then. The biggest thing was to know that I could stop and not feel guilty about it because the world wouldn't fall apart.

Question #7—Am I Putting First Things First? (Because *Most* Kids Are Only in a Fourth-Grade Christmas Play Once)

Every year at Bayside, we prepare several massive Christmas Eve services. It's the biggest thing we do all year. Bigger than the demanding Easter season. In fact, last year, more than forty thousand people showed up for fourteen Christmas Eve services. I mean, it's a big deal to the whole community and a whole lot of fun.

Our worship pastor, Lincoln Brewster, is one of the biggest names in contemporary Christian music. He's the consummate professional and unbelievably God-gifted. Lots of people come just to hear *him*, not me. Lots of visitors come for the first time because someone said, "You have to *hear* this guy!" He's that good and that integral to everything we do.

Two years ago, just before the Christmas season got crazy, Lincoln came up to me and said, "I'm trying to figure something out. My son is in a school play that takes place during our first Christmas Eve performance. I'll be at our service, I'll do all my stuff, and then I'll race over there to see part of his play, then I'll come back."

"No, you're not," I said without a second's thought.

"W-what?"

"Have someone else lead the *whole* service," I said. "Matter of fact, if you're at that service during your son's play, you're fired. Go watch the play. We'll handle it."

Tears sprang up in his eyes. "Are you *serious*?"

"Yes," I said. "We'll handle it. We'll have more services, and you'll be there for all of them. But don't show up for the first one."

I had an immediate answer because I knew that Lincoln's son would remember his play a lot longer than anyone would remember the service.

Reminds me of the guy I once heard about who habitually brought work home with him.

His kindergarten daughter asked, "Daddy, why do you always bring work home?"

"Because I just don't get it finished at work," he said.

"Daddy," the girl said with a sweet smile. "Maybe they should put you in a slower group."[12]

Lincoln walked into the school auditorium that evening right before the play started, and his son saw him. The boy beamed and waved. Lincoln stayed for the whole performance. He and his son made it to church that night, arriving at the very end of the service. We had the two of them come out and lead the traditional candle lighting. It was *so* cool. Both Lincoln and his son still talk about it. We definitely raised their Hope Quotient that night.

If Lincoln hadn't taken the drastic action, I would have done it for him. Don't allow things to get drastic. *You* get drastic and put first things first.

What Is at Stake?

One by one, Carol and I watched our children go away to college, until our youngest kids, twin daughters, left. Carol and I spent a wonderful weekend with them and then dropped them off at Azusa Pacific University. It was the single hardest thing I've ever done. At two o'clock on a Sunday afternoon, we gathered under an oak tree and took pictures, and I choked on my words as I said, "In four years when you graduate you will stand underneath this oak tree and we'll take another family picture with you and your diplomas."

I got even more misty-eyed as we put our arms around each other, prayed, and told each other what we appreciated about one another. Then, for the first time in my life, I watched them walk away. They followed a path to their dorm rooms, while Carol and I walked the other way to our car. It felt like the worst moment of my life.

We pulled out of the driveway and made it about three blocks before I was crying so hard I couldn't see. I pulled into a parking lot, and Carol and I just sat there holding each other and crying. After about fifteen minutes, I finally dried my eyes. I looked up and saw we had pulled into a bank parking lot. Then I thought about how much college was going to cost and cried for another five minutes.

Once we pulled ourselves together, we prayed again for our daughters. Instead of going straight home, we went to Newport Beach and spent the next three days staying with friends. On the second afternoon, I was in their backyard when something dawned on me that I never saw coming. I realized I had no regrets.

Now, you need to understand, I am a world-class regretter. I regret everything. I regret I didn't sell my house ten years ago and then buy it back. I regret not buying Apple stock in 1995.

But with my daughters, we vacationed, I coached their basketball teams, we talked every day, and I thought, *I will be forever grateful for the people in my life who were on my back to make sure I put first things first.*

I didn't do it anywhere near perfectly, but if this chapter helps you put your most important relationships first on your schedule, those people will then be first in your heart. You will have fewer regrets and much more gratitude. That's hope where it matters.

11.

SEVEN: PLAY GREAT DEFENSE

Finally, be strong in the Lord and in his mighty power. Put on the full armor of God so that you can take your stand against the devil's schemes.

EPHESIANS 6:10–11

Be faithful in small things because it is in them that your strength lies.

MOTHER TERESA

It was hot and muggy when I landed in Florida, where I'd accepted an invitation to speak at a beautiful conference center located on a lake. I decided to go straight out for a swim, so I walked down to the dock. I saw no one swimming, but I did see one old codger rocking in a weathered chair. He looked like something out of *Duck Dynasty*—a man with a lot of facial hair and few words.

"Looks like a pretty hot day," I said.

"Yep," he said.

"Is it like this a lot here?"

"Yep."

"Live here a long time?"

"Yep."

I turned my back on the chatterbox, took off my shirt, and was just getting ready to dive in when Mr. Personality actually said a complete sentence.

"I wouldn't do that."

"Really? Why not? Is it against conference center rules or something?"

"Nope."

I just stood there, waiting to know *why*. He finally said, "You're about to dive into the number two most alligator-infested lake in the state of Florida."

I hadn't noticed anything dangerous, but when I turned around to look again, I saw somewhere between eight and twelve gators, some as close as fifteen feet from the dock . . . all staring straight at *me*. And you know what they were thinking: *Lunch!*

"Thanks, man," I said, scrambling back into my shirt. "Is this *really* the number two most alligator-infested lake in Florida?"

It seemed as though the man wanted to teach this California boy a lesson. He looked me straight in the eyes and said, "Yep. Number two most infested lake."

He paused, then grinned and said, "But it only takes *one*."

In this chapter, I am going to describe some of the chief predators that kill hope and destroy dreams. Each one is so deadly that it can take you out, wreck your marriage, ruin your life, destroy your church, or torch your business. It only takes *one*.

Hope Killers

After I began to follow Christ, I started reading the Bible (sounded like a good idea). Eventually I came to what, for me, is the most surprising verse in the Bible. In Hebrews 11, God's "hall of faith" celebrates and profiles a bunch of incredible men and women of faith and holds them up as examples for us to follow.

The next chapter starts with the word "therefore," so I thought, *Okay, here's the application verse to one of the most important chapters in the Bible.* But that next verse didn't say what I thought it would say. "Therefore," the verse says, "since we are surrounded by such a great cloud of witnesses, let us . . ." and I thought it would say, "let us pray," or "let us study the Bible," or "let us give money away." But the writer startled me. He finished instead with "let us throw off everything that hinders and the sin that so easily entangles" (Hebrews 12:1).

I was shocked that day to discover that if we desire to be spiritually healthy and walk with God in any effective way, then job number one is to let go of anything toxic. Whatever has the power to kill faith, hope, and our spiritual lives, we must unload. Most of these hope killers operate according to a simple but deadly principle: *Sin fascinates, then assassinates.*

"If you want to be a person of hope," God tells us, "you have to let go of everything toxic."

During Easter week one year, I served in Mexico with five thousand students from all around the United States. The kids worked in remote villages, giving wheelchairs to disabled people who could never afford them. They helped eye doctors in free clinics and all kinds of other initiatives, all designed to give hope where it was needed.

I spoke one night to these students about the power of letting things go. I said, "If you're ever going to have a healthy, alive walk with God, then you have got to let go of some things." I talked about bitterness and anger and being anchored to a toxic past.

"In a group this size," I said, "some of you came down here and are abusing alcohol or drugs and they'll take you down roads you don't want to travel. You may have brought them to Mexico. If that's you, here's what I want you to do. Tonight, receive God's forgiveness and a fresh start. Then take your drugs and throw them into the *baño* [that's Spanish for stinky-outhouse-standing-in-the-hot-sun-too-long]. Later, if you need that stuff so bad that you're tempted to try to reach down and retrieve it, then come see me, because you've really got a problem."

About fifteen minutes later, around eleven at night, I stood in a dirt field talking with some of the adults when I saw three teenagers waiting to speak with me. I found out later one was a junior, another a sophomore, and the third a freshman in high school. I walked up to them, and the oldest guy spoke up.

"All three of us gave our lives to Christ tonight. But there's something we've got to get rid of." He paused and said, "Here," then handed me a huge stash of marijuana.

I walked those teenagers over to the *baño*, opened the door, and watched them throw that stuff away. Then, under a beautiful full moon in Mexico at eleven thirty at night, I wrapped my arms around three young teenagers and prayed for them and their futures. As I watched them walk back to their tents and their teams, into a whole different future, I thought, *Those teenagers have just saved themselves and their parents from a lifetime of heartache.*

Sin does fascinate, then it does assassinate.

Let me give you five of the most toxic hope killers on the planet.

HK1 *1. Bitterness and resentment*

Bitterness and the resentment that follows are nothing but emotional suicide. They poison you and everyone around you. Resentment will not only kill you but also make you crazy first.

Sonya married as a teenager. Before the wedding, her husband-to-be, famed author Leo Tolstoy, insisted that she read his diaries because he wanted her to know what kind of man he had been before the marriage. The diaries contained countless details about many lurid liaisons. Sonya never forgave Leo for what he'd done. Resentment poisoned her life.

She felt especially bitter about one of his former lovers, a woman named Axinya, who lived in their village. Sonya saw Axinya every day and would write vicious notes in her diary about the woman. Sonya refused to forgive, and a bitter root kept growing in her soul. She wrote, "One of these days I shall kill myself with jealousy. . . . He relishes that peasant wench with her strong female body and her sunburnt legs, she allures him just as powerfully now as she did all those years ago."

Sonya wrote those words when both she and Axinya had climbed well past eighty years of age. She could see nothing in that shriveled eighty-year-old woman but the suntanned legs and shapely body that had long ago disappeared.[1]

Resentment is completely illogical that way. One episode of the old radio program *Amos and Andy* featured a man who kept hitting Amos on the chest until Amos couldn't stand it any longer. Amos complained to Andy one day,

"I know what I'm going to do. I'm going to stop that guy from hitting me. I'm going to strap some dynamite onto my chest, and then the next time he slaps me, he's going to get his hand blown off!"[2]

It's been said that resentment is like taking poison and waiting for the other person to die. Resentment always hurts you more than it does whoever hurt you.

"Watch out that no poisonous root of bitterness grows up to trouble you, corrupting many" (Hebrews 12:15 NLT).

Bitterness is emotional suicide and a murderer of hope. Let it go.

HK2 *2. Worry and anxiety*

Warren Wiersbe, the prolific Christian author and leader, declared, "Most Christians are being crucified on a cross between two thieves: yesterday's regrets and tomorrow's worries."[3]

Worry is utterly worthless. It can't change the past. It can't control the future. All it does is make you miserable today. Worrying has been connected to high blood pressure, heart trouble, blindness, migraines, thyroid malfunctions, and a host of stomach disorders. Dr. Alexis Carrel, winner of the Nobel Peace Prize in medicine, said, "People who don't know how to fight worry die young!"[4] It's like the hypochondriac who put on his tombstone, "I told you I was sick."

Corrie ten Boom reminded us, "Worry does not empty tomorrow of its sorrow, it empties today of its strength."[5]

Do you know that Jesus, in the Sermon on the Mount, had more to say about worry than about any other topic? He gave more attention to worry than to prayer, giving, fasting, or any other issue. That amazes me. God's Son comes to earth, and in His first major sermon, the topic He chooses to hammer home is the hope killer of worry.

I take note of that, because anyone who grew up in my house had good reason to worry. My CEO dad, a former football player, stood six foot three and shaped me in many wonderful ways. I will always be grateful for the positive things he built into my life. Until I was ten years old, I thought of my dad as a rock star. Then, a frightening pattern began. A combination of alcohol and anger did not do good things to my dad. I learned to walk on eggshells. As soon as I got home, my anxiety level skyrocketed. First, I would have to find my dad to figure out if everything was going to be okay. If so, I could relax. If not, I would stress about how to fix it. I remember many times when my two younger sisters crept into my room after our parents started fighting. I'd take the screen off my window, hop out, help them out, and take them on a walk, just to get away.

With this family background, by the time I became a Christian I was pretty good at worrying. It didn't just stop with family things. I worried about grades, finances, health. You name it, I could stress out about it. This is why this verse means more to me than I can describe: "Cast all your anxiety on him because he cares for you" (1 Peter 5:7).

After reading this verse, I started a pattern that finally broke the grip that fear and anxiety had on my spirit. Every night before I went to bed, I sat in a chair in my living room and reread the verse: "Cast all your anxiety on him because he cares for you." Then I would think of all the issues around me and say, "All right, God. That's Yours. That's Yours. That's Yours . . ." It felt like shooting hoops. I would keep casting them on Him. "That's Yours. That's Yours . . ." Then I'd finish by saying, "Okay, You have to handle this stuff. I'm going to bed."

You may think, *That sounds too easy.* But the verse and that simple prayer of faith broke the grip of anxiety and stress in my life that I thought was impossible to break.

George Müller once said, "The beginning of anxiety is the end of faith. The beginning of true faith is the end of anxiety."[6]

Anxiety won't just weaken your life; it will shorten it. Let it go.

HK3 3. Looking back and comparing

Some people have rearview mirrors that are bigger than their car windshields. I have a 1965 Mustang convertible. It's really a cool car. When you think about it, there's not much from the past *worth* keeping except a '65 Mustang. One Sunday, I decided to take the rearview mirror to church with me. I unscrewed it, got to church, held it up for everyone to see, and said, "See this? This is a great device to use when you're driving, but it is a lousy thing to have as part of your life for living. Good for driving, bad for living!"

Some people spend their entire lives looking in their rearview mirrors. "I wish this person hadn't done that to me." "I wish my parents had done this." "I wish I had done that." Their whole view of the future is clouded, and they are chained by their pasts. That isn't even living.

Looking back is a terrible strategy for developing your gifts and pursuing your dreams. Looking back and comparing rather than looking ahead and dreaming just devastates hope.

Sometimes we need to learn from guys smarter than us. General Colin Powell, the former United States secretary of state, had a reporter ask him once if he had any regrets. General Powell looked at the reporter and gave a brilliant answer. He said, "What good are regrets? Regrets slow you down. Regrets cause you to fail to pay attention to the future. So I never log, count, or inventory my regrets. I move on."[7]

Man, that's good, isn't it?

That stuff in your rearview mirror? Let it go.

HK4 *4. Guilt*

Do you know anyone wracked with guilt who feels the slightest sense of hope? I don't. The Bible is clear about this—the minute you place your faith in Christ, you are forgiven and freed from your past. Need a reminder? Here are a few:

- You are forgiven (1 John 1:9).
- There is no condemnation for you (Romans 8:1).
- Your past doesn't matter (Philippians 3:13).
- You will never be separated from the love of God (Romans 8:35–39).

You're in the family of God. You're a son! You're a daughter! You have all the rights of a child of God, adopted into His family by grace through your faith in Christ.

Think of it like this. I am a dad to four kids. How would I feel, as a parent, if my son came home and said, "Oh, Dad, I'm not worthy to be called your son. Just let me live in the garage. Let me eat the crumbs off your table"? While from a financial perspective this might seem like an excellent idea, I wouldn't hear of it. I'd pick him up, straighten his shoulders, and say, "What are you talking about? You're my son. Get in here! Eat with us. Live with us. And start acting like you're part of this family, because you are."

We honor God most when we say, "God, I know I'm Your child. I know I'm forgiven through my faith in Christ. I believe You have great things in store for me, and I am choosing to let go of my past."

I *like* it when my children face the world with confidence. I *like* it when they feel they're something special. I *like* it when they get home from school and go straight to the fridge. They don't ask for permission. They don't beg, "Oh most beneficent Father, thou who feedeth us, clotheth us, and provideth for our every need, I beseech thee, can I have a Coke?" That would be crazy. They march in there like they own the place. Why? Because they know they're part of our family.

If you're ever going to become the person God intended you to be, you need that same strong sense of confidence. Without it, guilt will assassinate your hope and leave you muttering in the dark. Let it go.

`HK5` *5. Past failures*

The team that makes the most mistakes is usually the one that wins, because their mistakes mean they're trying something.

John Wooden, the famous UCLA college basketball coach with the most men's championship banners in history, never let failure keep him from reaching toward success. "If you're not making mistakes," he said, "then you're not doing anything. I'm positive that a doer makes mistakes."[8]

Johnny Cash, the famous singer who battled serious drug and alcohol abuse, said, "You build on failure. You use it as a stepping stone. Close the door on the past. You don't try to forget the mistakes, but you don't dwell on it. You don't let it have any of your energy, or any of your time, or any of your space."[9]

I love what Mike Yaconelli used to say: "Quit worrying about your failures. They are simply speed bumps on the road to better days."[10]

Every hope-filled, thriving, successful person has two things in common:

1. They have a lot of past failures.
2. They never let those past failures stop them.

"Forgetting the past and looking forward to what lies ahead," the apostle Paul wrote, "I strain to reach the end of the race and receive the prize for which God, through Christ Jesus, is calling us" (Philippians 3:13–14 NLT). Keep in mind that this is the same guy who called himself the "worst of sinners" (1 Timothy 1:16) and who said he did "not even deserve to be called an apostle" (1 Corinthians 15:9) because of his violent past. Paul remembered his past, but he didn't let it chain him to guilt. He let it go.

Do the same. Let it go.

Any of these five hope killers, like alligators, can take you out. The real question is this: When some of them surface, are there any practical steps you can take to improve your defense? Let me give you three life strategies I've learned over a lifetime. All three of these are major life lessons.

Life Strategy #1—Never Make Decisions When You're Down

Shortly after I became a Christian, I had to deal with some difficult, painful circumstances. My parents separated, college was more expensive than I thought, my car broke down almost every time I drove it, and I had serious doubts that the "abundant life" promises included me. I walked into where my friend and early mentor Jon Archer was sitting and threw my Bible across the room.

"I'm done," I said.

Jon saved my life with one line. He looked at me with compassion and said, "Never make decisions when you're down.

"If I made decisions while I was down, I wouldn't be married," he said. "If I made decisions when I was down, I wouldn't have kids. If I made decisions when I was down, I would have quit my job. If I made decisions when I was down, I wouldn't have my faith.

"The single most important thing any human being needs to do is to determine that they, for the rest of their life, will not make any decisions when they're down."

Let's be honest: human beings are wired so the minute we get down, we start making decisions. "I quit." "I'm leaving." "I'm moving." "I'm walking out." "I'm giving somebody a piece of my mind." Almost all knee-jerk decisions end up being destructive decisions. Jon's counsel changed my life. The incident took place thirty-five years ago, but the lesson still keeps me from destroying my hope.

Don't make decisions when you're down. Decisions determine direction, which determines destiny. In other words, the decisions you make determine the direction you take. The direction you take determines your destiny. Everything you are, everything you will be, is due to the decisions you will make.

Life Strategy #2—Respond to Bad News in Great Ways

I used to think there were dozens of keys to successful living, but a few years ago God changed my mind. He used Nehemiah to teach me something we mentioned a few chapters back. It bears explaining a bit more because if we don't use *this* key, we won't be around long enough to use any of the other keys.

As I reread the story of Nehemiah, it dawned on me that the Hebrews living in Jerusalem had for ninety-two years responded to bad news in bad ways. The Babylonians had devastated the land of Judah, leaving Jerusalem in ruins and without a protective wall. Because God's people responded to the bad news in bad ways, they continued to spiral down.

The book of Nehemiah begins with bad news, a depressing report: "Those who survived the exile and are back in the province are in great trouble and disgrace. The wall of Jerusalem is broken down, and its gates have been burned with fire" (Nehemiah 1:3). Nehemiah breaks down into tears and mourns for days. He gets down but doesn't stay there. He prays, catches fresh vision, moves to Jerusalem, and then springs into action. Fifty-two days later, a new wall of protection had been built and Jerusalem had a bright new future. One guy responded to bad news in great ways and it changed *everything*.

The number one key to success in anything is to respond to bad news in great ways. If you do that, you'll have a future. If you do that, your family will have a future. If you do that, your kids will have a future. If you do that, your church will have a future. If enough people do that, their country could have a brighter future. No one is going to do well over a decade if they don't respond to bad news in great ways.

The great American inventor Thomas Edison started more than one hundred companies before the age of forty and held more than one thousand patents that changed the way the world works. His inventions of the incandescent lightbulb, the phonograph, and a viable motion picture system continue to shape our planet today. He lived by a set of core principles, among them a determination to never give up.

That determination got severely tested on December 9, 1914, when an explosion and fire leveled his corporate campus in West Orange, New Jersey. "Edison Sees His Vast Plan Burn," shouted the headline in the *New York Times*. Edison was there when the fire started and directed efforts to save as much as possible, but the loss amounted to about $7 million, which would be well over $100 million today.

"Although I am over 67 years old," he told a *Times* reporter, "I'll start all over again tomorrow. I am pretty well burned out tonight, but tomorrow there will be a mobilization here and the debris will be cleared away, if it is cooled sufficiently, and I will go right to work to reconstruct the plant."

Edison's determination was all the more remarkable because he made the statement in the middle of the disaster, according to the reporter, "as he watched the flames destroy building after building."[11]

Sometime after the catastrophe, Edison declared, "There is great value in disaster. All our mistakes are burned up. Thank God we can start anew."[12]

And start anew he did. During the fire, Edison noted how the loss of power and light had hampered firefighters, so he designed a portable, battery-powered searchlight with a three-million-candlepower beam. Within six months, he demonstrated his invention to astonished visitors at a nearby park.

When you respond to bad news in great ways, who knows what the future might hold?

Life Strategy #3—Shake It Off and Step Up

An old parable tells of a farmer who owned a mule that fell into an abandoned, dry well. The farmer decided that neither the mule nor the well were worth saving, so he enlisted his neighbors to help haul dirt to bury the old mule in the well and put him out of his misery. The old mule brayed hysterically as the first shovels of dirt rained down on him. But as he struggled, a thought struck the mule. *Every time a shovel of dirt lands on my back*, he thought, *I'll just shake it off and step up.* So that's what he did. Shovelful after shovelful, the old mule fought panic and just kept right on shaking it off and stepping up. *Shake it off and step up!* he kept thinking. *Shake it off and step up!* Before long, the battered and exhausted mule stepped triumphantly over the wall of that well and into a new chance at life.

We can learn a lot from that old mule. If we refuse to let regret, bitterness, worry, failures, and the guilt that rains down on us bury us, then those things have within them the power to lift us to levels we've never before reached. If we refuse to let the hope killers steal our future and bury us, then we set ourselves up for something great that God wants to do through us.

One of the great comeback stories in Scripture is Joseph. He was betrayed, sold into slavery, wrongfully accused, and imprisoned, but he was able to look those hope killers in the eye and say, "You intended to harm me, but God intended it for good" (Genesis 50:20).

That's playing great defense. And that's what we need to do if we want

God-size hope to energize our marriages, our children, our churches, our careers, and even our communities.

The "Shake It Off and Step Up" chart means so much to me that I passed it out to everyone who attended our church one weekend. The reason is, the last thing any community needs is ten thousand more people filled with resentment, fear, anxiety, and discouragement. We need to shake it off and step up.

Shake It Off (Don't Buy the Lie)	Step Up into Truth (Truth-Based Living)
Resentment—I can't forgive.	"I can do all things through Christ who strengthens me." Philippians 4:13 NKJV
Fear—I'm filled with insecurity.	"God has not given us a spirit of fear, but of power and of love and of a sound mind." 2 Timothy 1:7 NKJV
Anxiety—I can't relax.	"Cast all your anxiety on [Christ] because he cares for you." 1 Peter 5:7 "Do not be anxious about anything." Philippians 4:6
Discouragement—I'm ready to give up.	"This I call to mind and therefore I have hope: Because of the LORD's great love we are not consumed, for his compassions never fail. They are new every morning; great is your faithfulness." Lamentations 3:21–23 "Let us not become weary in doing good, for at the proper time we will reap a harvest if we do not give up." Galatians 6:9
Isolation—I am all alone.	"I [the Lord] will never leave you nor forsake you." Hebrews 13:5 NKJV
Guilt—I am filled with shame.	"There is now no condemnation for those who are in Christ Jesus." Romans 8:1
Failure—I can't picture future success.	"In all these things we are more than conquerors through him who loved us." Romans 8:37
Stress—I am overwhelmed by life's pressures.	"In the world you will have tribulation; but be of good cheer, I have overcome the world." John 16:33 NKJV

Weary—I am weak and exhausted.	"The LORD is the strength of my life." Psalm 27:1 NKJV
Opposition—I am under attack from the enemy.	"The one who is in you is greater than the one who is in the world." 1 John 4:4
Confusion—I lack wisdom and don't know what to do.	"God generously gives wisdom to those who ask him for it." James 1:5, author's paraphrase
Lack of faith—I lack financial resources.	"My God shall supply all your need according to His riches in glory by Christ Jesus." Philippians 4:19 NKJV

PART THREE

UNLEASHING A CULTURE OF HOPE

12.

UNLEASHING HOPE IN YOUR MARRIAGE

Let marriage be held in honor (esteemed worthy, precious, of great price, and especially dear).

HEBREWS 13:4 AMP

Incompatibility is grounds for a great marriage!

CHUCK AND BARB SYNDER

This is a chapter I *never* thought I would write. Divorce in my family isn't just a reality; my family treated it like a *requirement*. My parents divorced. Their parents all divorced. All of their siblings divorced. All of their kids divorced. All of my siblings have now divorced. In our family history, not one lasting marriage existed—until now. Carol and I just celebrated our thirtieth anniversary.

I love it when a skeptic tries to challenge me with, "I don't believe the Christian faith makes any discernable difference." Or, "This stuff about hope isn't strong or deep enough to really change anything."

Living for Jesus Christ and living with hope makes all the difference in the world.

For married readers, and those who intend to be married, this might be the most important chapter in this book. Pass it on to those you love because, let's face it, marriages are in deep trouble. American marriages especially. Consider a few alarming statistics:

- Fifty percent of all marriages end in divorce.
- There are 6,646 divorces every day.
- Forty-one percent of first marriages end in divorce.
- Sixty percent of second marriages end in divorce.
- Seventy-three percent of third marriages end in divorce.[1]

American homes and families are breaking down in record numbers without a great deal of public outrage and action. Very few seem bent on trying to stop this epidemic. One reason I decided to write about hope is that during thirty years of marriage, during thirty years of breaking past family patterns, during thirty years of working with couples, I have reached a startling conclusion:

Hope is the greatest antidote against the toxic forces that are destroying American homes.

Any marriage can be stronger. *Any* marriage can be closer. *Any* marriage can be more stable. How do you build a marriage to last a lifetime? By building a solid, hope-based foundation. Let me show you five ways to do it.

1. Give Up Unrealistic Expectations

One pastor described it this way:

> Incredible expectations for marriage begin the minute a couple starts planning the wedding. Have you ever read a "bride" magazine? They ought to be classified under "science fiction." All the women's blemishes and flaws have been airbrushed out. No one is ugly. Everybody, guests included, are stunning in those magazines.
>
> As a pastor, I have been involved in some weddings that took on Disney extravaganza proportions with a cast of thousands, building up to a forty-five minute event. The woman is hibernated for three days and turns into a goddess that walks down an aisle. It's a fantasy world of everything-must-be-perfect. The honeymoon is some far-off place that nobody could

afford to go to. But it's going to be perfect. There are no mosquitoes or sunburns there.

Fast forward about six months. The same couple is sitting around the breakfast table. The guy's in a t-shirt with a day's stubble. She has yesterday's mascara smeared down her face. They're arguing over how come they can't meet the budget and who's going to take out the garbage. They're looking at each other and saying, "What happened?"[2]

The problem is that we can bring such high expectations into marriage that no person could possibly meet them. That sets us up for disappointment followed by discouragement followed by despair. We start saying, "Maybe I made a mistake. Maybe I married the wrong person. Why didn't I listen to my mother?"

The reality is that marriage is composed of two very flawed, very imperfect individuals. It is crazy to think that two imperfect individuals can form one flawless, problem-free relationship. It's just an unrealistic expectation.

2. Give Up Hollywood's Myths of Marriage

In Proverbs we read, "There is a way that seems right to a man, but its end is the way of death" (16:25 NKJV). I like movies. Carol and I go a lot. But almost every time I see a romantic comedy, I want to stand up in the theater and shout, "*You have got to be kidding*!" They might seem right, but these Hollywood myths lead to death. They are guaranteed to turn romance into resentment.

The myth of compatibility

Every couple Carol and I have counseled that has opted for divorce has said the same thing: "We are just not [wait for it, now] compatible." News flash—*no one is!* If you two agree about everything, one of you is not necessary.

Carol and I are about as incompatible as it gets. You've heard that opposites attract. Well, after marriage, opposites attack. She got so frustrated one time she made a list of how opposite we are. Here's what she wrote:

I am an early morning person. Ray is a late night person.

Ray is a visionary. I'm a realist.

Ray has lots of ideas. I have lots of
reasons why they won't work.

I like to stop and smell the roses. Ray is
driving so fast he runs over them.

I like hamburgers with everything on them. Ray likes them plain.

To relax I engage in conversation. To relax Ray disengages.

Ray likes to spend money. I like to save it.

Ray likes to give money away. I don't.

I like to sit down at a restaurant and
relax. Ray likes the drive-through.

Ray likes to speak. I like to listen.

Ray goes into a room and talks to dozens of
people. I go in and talk to two or three.

Ray is the life of a party. I just like to organize it.

I have grown as a husband, as a father, as a person, and as a Christian primarily by being married to someone who is *different* from me. My life is richer, my relationships are deeper, and I am healthier because I married someone who forced me out of my self-centered comfort zone.

Paul Tournier wrote in *To Understand Each Other*,

> So called "emotional incompatibility" is a myth invented by jurists short of arguments in order to plead for divorce. It is likewise a common excuse people use in order to hide their own failings.
>
> I simply do not believe it exists. There are no emotional incompatibilities. There are misunderstandings and mistakes, however, which can be corrected when there is a willingness to do so. The issue is not incompatibility; the issue is selfishness, stubbornness, unwilling to compromise, unwilling to change, unwilling to work to save the relationship. Don't call it incompatibility, call it what it is—self-centeredness.[3]

Paul Popenoe wrote in *Marriage Is What You Make It*, "Incompatibility—it would be hard to find a word that is so often used so unscientifically. Almost any two people are compatible if they try to be so."[4]

Hope-based people believe that marriage is what they make of it. They say, "No matter how different we may be, our marriage will become what we are both committed to making it."

The myth of smooth sailing

We see all these movies where the Prince Charming shows up and sets the fair maiden free, and they ride into the sunset on a white horse to live happily ever after as the credits roll. If you think you are riding off into the sunset where I live, check again. It's probably smog. Any "riding into the sunset" script is not reality.

Even our process today for dating, courtship, engagement, wedding, and honeymoon is a setup for massive disappointment. In no other area of life do we place such high expectations. When dating, people act like no one does in normal life. They wear their best clothes all the time, are on their best behavior, and spend extravagantly for things they don't have money to buy.

A friend of mine gave some brilliant advice to a twenty-year-old. He said, "You're in your twenties, and you want to buy a diamond? How many people in their twenties really need a diamond? What you need is a car, a job, and a place to live!"

The problem in living a fantasy and expecting smooth sailing is that we are unprepared for the storms when they hit.

The myth of greener pastures

People falling for this myth use two words: *if only. If only* they were . . . (Fill in the blank: taller, smarter, kinder, thinner, more communicative . . .) The list is endless. Robert Fulghum wrote in his brilliant bestseller *It Was on Fire When I Lay Down on It*, "The grass is not, in fact, always greener on the other side of the fence. . . . Fences have nothing to do with it. The grass is greenest where it is watered. When crossing over fences, carry water with you and tend the grass wherever you may be."[5]

Hope-based couples shift from *comparing* to *cultivating*. They stop comparing their mates to everybody else: "If she/he were more like . . ." Instead, they start cultivating. They water their own relationships and watch them grow, watch them develop, watch them expand and become all that God wants them to be.

The myth that positive change is impossible

Jesus put it this way: "With men this is impossible, but with God all things are possible" (Matthew 19:26 NKJV). Right now you may be confused about your marriage. You may be disappointed in your marriage. You may be feeling that your marriage is hopeless.

Jason and Renee Krogh married at age twenty-four and got pregnant four months later. Two years later, Renee started to crave a spiritual foundation for her growing family. Jason's position was, "I don't like church." Instead, he focused on his career, becoming an executive in the semiconductor industry in his late twenties, jetting all over the world. Within a decade, the couple had four children but had grown apart.

"I was rubbing shoulders with billionaires who could fly anywhere they wanted on their Gulfstreams," Jason said. "It was intoxicating. I thought, *This is what I want. My family is getting in my way. It's best if we just divorce.*"

One night at the Mandalay Bay VIP room in Las Vegas, Jason took note of the people surrounding him, including "a whole slew of celebrities. I looked to my left and saw this guy who had been married four or five times. I looked at the next guy, addicted to alcohol and drugs. I looked at the next guy, whose son had died of a drug overdose. It hit me: These were my mentors? I thought, *This just can't be my drive, my life. This is ridiculous.*"

Jason had already told Renee that he wanted a divorce. When he returned home, she said, "We can divorce and you can chase these things you want, but you know how your life is going to end up. Or we can go find God."

Some praying women who surrounded Renee had helped keep a spark of hope alive. Renee said, "I knew what Jason was lacking. I wanted to get that for him, I wanted to get that for *us*. I was not willing to take the easy road and grab my kids and leave. We just had to find the common denominator for us to start building a better life and a better marriage."

Jason finally agreed to visit a church that met in a high school gym. As an athlete, he didn't think he could get "struck by lightning" there. He kept going, eventually accepted Christ, got baptized, and even joined a men's Bible study. "That scared me to death, walking into that room for the first time with my brand-new Bible in my hand. I got around men who were struggling and trying to figure out the same things I was. They weren't all Bible-thumping geeks, but real guys with real lives. That had a huge impact on me."

Eventually, Jason's company wanted to promote him to general manager. At age forty-two, he had a big decision to make. He had felt a strong pull toward ministry after his conversion and had volunteered many hours. He believed God might be leading him down that road, but could he trust God enough to make the jump?

In July 2012, Jason resigned from his company and joined the Bayside staff full time. On the eve of their twentieth anniversary, both Jason and Renee described their lives as "blessed," "awesome," and "purposeful." Renee noted, "Bottom line, it just takes an ounce of hope. It just takes one ounce to keep you going from one day to the next."

None of this would have happened without hope. When hope enters, it brings all the possibilities that change can happen.

3. Give Up "Fixing" the Blame and Start Solving the Problem

Blame is deadly. I'll never forget a young couple who came into my office years ago, seeking counsel for their troubled marriage. They looked sharp; they had two beautiful young children, a gorgeous home, and scowls that blistered the paint on my office walls.

"What's up?" I asked. That's all it took.

"Well, *he* . . ." She took off and shredded the guy for what seemed like thirty minutes. Then she made a strategic mistake—she took a breath. He took over. "Well, *she* . . ." Out came a machine gun of hurtful words that riddled her. Back and forth they went, with increasing volume until staff members stationed outside my office left to work at the loud coffee shop around the corner because it was quieter.

"Just shut up for a minute," I finally said. (I've mentioned that counseling isn't my forte, haven't I?) "You two might be the single most immature pair of adults I have ever met, and I can prove it! Your children are about six and eight years old, right?"

"Yeah."

"Would you let your son talk to your daughter the way you just talked about her?"

The husband slumped in his chair. The wife got pale and quiet.

"You don't even have the maturity of six-year-olds," I said. Then I was struck with a thought. "Come back another time when you are ready to *fix the problem* instead of just trying to '*fix*' *the blame*."

You cannot fix the blame and solve the problem at the same time. That couple was suffering the consequences of a life without hope. Without hope, people do not believe things can improve. Discouraged people become destructive people. Blame takes the place of hope and fills the home (and my office) with all kinds of toxic emotions. The two of them had arrived with enough ammunition to destroy each other for hours. Eventually, those two made changes, and the last I heard, their kids grew up unscathed by divorce.

Without hope, people become disillusioned and discouraged, but people with hope believe that things actually can get better. Hope leads to the type of actions that lead to things getting better.

4. Give Up Focusing on Yourself

It's pretty simple—marriages grow from attention and suffer from neglect. I tell every couple whose wedding I officiate the same story. On my wedding day, my pastor gave me three words that summarize what the Bible teaches about marriage. Taken seriously, a marriage can last a lifetime filled with *fun*, *faith*, and *faithfulness*. I engrave those words on matching silver key chains, one for each of them, and tell them that I'm going to test them on those words after the honeymoon. Then I explain.

1. Play together.

If you play together, you will make your marriage *fun*. Life will make you uptight, so make laughter the number one sound in your home. Cemeteries are filled with people who are dead serious about life. Keep dating! Get out of town! Plan vacations! Get hobbies! Goof off! Figure out what you like to do and get after it. *Fun* is a great atmosphere to have in a home. Kids will love it. Your faith and values will be far more attractive to the world and to your own kids when they see you actually enjoying God and life!

2. Pray together.

If you pray together, you will build your *faith*. The closer you grow to God, the closer you will grow toward each other. Get connected to God. Get connected to a thriving church. Get connected to God's Word. What difference does it make? When you are forgiven by God, you will have grace to give each other. When you receive encouragement from God, you have hope to give each other. When you receive power from God, you have strength to give each other. God-connected people have resources flowing into their homes that other people only dream of.

3. Stay together.

Make a lasting commitment to each other. If you stay together, you will create *faithfulness*. After all the years of divorce in my family, I am convinced *faith* that leads to *faithfulness* is the *best and only* solid foundation that will last a lifetime.

"If you do these three things," I tell the new couple, "you will have the kind of marriage that every person dreams of having. *Fun. Faith. Faithfulness.* With those three words, you'll be able to build something your children and grandchildren will benefit from for generations."

5. Refuse to Give Up

When a couple hits the wall, they break down, break up, or break through. People without hope say, "Nothing's going to work, so why even try?" When you become a person of hope, you are convinced that God has better days ahead, and that you can become the one who breaks through.

I've chopped down my own family tree, and Carol and I have used it for kindling to build a brand-new family. Hope believes that a new, healthy family tree can start right here, right now. That reminds me of David and Cindee.

David Durham grew up essentially without a father. His dad, a high-powered attorney, left the family during David's toddler years and married five more times, the last wife being the same age as David. David remembered attending his grandfather's funeral when he was about ten. At the cemetery, his father left him in the car, but David could still see his father across the parking lot, heartbroken and sobbing.

"I couldn't understand why he would be so upset that his dad died," David said. "I had no reference for that. I didn't know what having a dad who cared about you was even like."

David grew up, got an apartment and a job, and moved in with Cindee. Cindee also lacked any good role models for a successful relationship.

"We had no example whatsoever of a healthy marriage," Cindee said. "We had never seen a healthy marriage that showed us how to relate to each other in a positive way."

They decided to get married, but after they did, David continued to live as though he were single. He stayed out late every night with buddies, playing pool and hanging out. David's mom saw the train wreck about to happen and insisted they accompany her to a traditional church. David didn't think that anyone had come to faith in that church for forty years, but one morning when a speaker gave "probably the worst sermon that's ever been preached," Cindee went to the front and gave her life to Christ. David and Cindee started listening to Christian programs on the radio and eventually tried out Bayside Church.

"Cindee and I walked in," David said, "looked at each other, and said, 'This is where we belong.'"

David also committed to Christ, got involved in a men's group, and for the first time in his life, saw what godly men do. Still, he had to fight against the example of his father. He never had an affair, but got involved enough to kiss another girl. Afterward, he was sitting in a Sunday service and heard a voice in his head say, *"She knows."* He thought, *There's no way*, but when he looked at Cindee again, he heard the voice again. *"She knows what happened."*

The couple went through some tumultuous times after that, but they refused to give up. They found a way to talk and developed communication skills. God put strong Christian role models in their lives. Finally, David realized he didn't have to follow his father's destructive path, and he and Cindee began to thrive as a couple.

Anyone's marriage can reflect their faith, not their background. You *can* beat the odds. *Any* couple can beat the odds. When you partner with hope, that strong and vibrant family tree can start with *you*. Just don't give up.

Beating the Odds

Belief in the power of hope to change struggling marriages flies in the face of what we see and hear all around us. Eric and Sabrina Walters have become believers.

Eric and Sabrina met in college one year after doctors told Sabrina she had two years to live. When they decided to marry anyway, Sabrina's oncologist urged them to plan not just a wedding but also her funeral. Her doctors made it clear that Eric was choosing to nurse her through a difficult and painful death. Eric and Sabrina placed their hope in God to make the time they would have together good time. They developed this vision statement for their marriage:

Our life is based in a strong and abiding faith in God. We will constantly steep our time in prayer, keep our home an open door, sacrificially give to others, and constantly grow in love and wisdom in every area of our lives.

Sabrina got pregnant, which doctors had said would kill both her and the baby. Instead, her blood counts shot to normal, baffling her physicians. She gave birth to a healthy baby boy. Then she got pregnant again, with the same result. Both times, her counts returned to their critical lows just hours after she gave birth. After she had a third son, Eric attended a church meeting where the speaker said, "Someone here needs to have a family member, who is not here, prayed for. That person needs healing."

The very conservative Eric was nonetheless drawn to that prayer and came home to tell Sabrina, "I prayed for you, and I think you might be healed."

Two weeks later, she visited her hematologist. With a puzzled expression, he clarified with her that she wasn't pregnant. Then he said, "It's weird because your counts are normal, just like when you're pregnant." The disease had gone into remission.

Sabrina researched what happened to her and now believes, "Love changes you. It changes your blood makeup, and since I had a blood disease, I think the stability of Eric's love and his constancy and basing our life in Christ physically changed me."

Ten years later, another crisis threatened their marriage. Sabrina went back into the workforce only to have an affair with her supervisor. Sabrina's father had abandoned her family after multiple affairs. She didn't want that same record of broken relationships. Neither she nor Eric wanted to give up on their union. They drew on the same hope that had seen them through her physical disease and fought to save their marriage. They pulled through.

"Hope is absolutely the bedrock of our relationship," Sabrina said. "Without it, we would have been sunk from the beginning."

Today, Sabrina is a licensed marriage and family counselor and therapist. (She says it cost sixty-two thousand dollars to get educated about what went wrong in her own heart.) She and Eric hold seminars through CoreValuesCouples.com to give couples hope and tools to grow a more intimate relationship and pull through betrayals and hardships. The Walterses call themselves "hope mongers." There's more. Because of their vision statement to keep an open door, they can now count fifty-four people who have lived with them for at least six weeks at a time, most of them staying a year.

"Hope comes forward through a fog of unbelief," Sabrina says today, "and then it becomes your new reality."

Do you want a burst of hope to infuse life and health throughout your marriage, regardless of your past and no matter your current circumstances? You have to go after it.

In another story I once read, a man named Tom Anderson came to understand that he had not pursued the health of his marriage nearly so much as he needed to. Because he wanted a new breeze of hope to flow through his home, he decided to go after it. So on a drive to a beach cottage to join his family for a two-week vacation, he made a vow to be a loving husband and father. He listened as he drove to a speaker quoting a Bible passage about husbands loving their wives.

The speaker said, "Love is an act of the will. A person can choose to love." For the first time, Tom admitted to himself that he'd been a selfish husband. He recalled the many times he'd chided his wife for her tardiness, insisted that he control the television channel, or thrown out newspapers before his wife, Evelyn, could read them. *All very petty*, he thought. But all of that was about to change.

He kissed Evelyn when she greeted him at the door and saw shock on her face when he said, "That new yellow sweater looks great on you."

Tom wanted to sit and read after his long drive, but Evelyn mentioned a walk on the beach. Just as he started to refuse, he thought, *Evelyn's been alone here with the kids all week and now she wants to be alone with me.* So the couple walked on the beach as their children flew kites.

For two weeks, he didn't call the Wall Street investment firm where he served as a director. He accompanied the family on a visit to a shell museum, although he despised museums. He held his tongue when Evelyn made them late for a dinner reservation. By the end of the vacation, Tom felt something he hadn't felt for a long time: relaxed and happy.

On the last night of their stay, Evelyn stared at her husband with deep sadness.

"What's the matter?" he asked her.

"Tom," she said, her voice full of worry, "do you know something I don't?"

"What do you mean?"

"Well . . . that checkup I had several weeks ago . . . our doctor . . . did he tell you something about me? Tom, you've been so good to me . . . *am I dying?*"

At first, Tom couldn't imagine what she meant. And then he burst out laughing.

"No, honey," he said, wrapping her in his arms, "you're not dying; I'm just starting to live!"[6]

Building anything, especially a lasting marriage, is not easy. And choosing hope over despair never is. But it's always worth it. A writer named Bob Benson died in 1986, but he captured one reason that a healthy, thriving, hope-filled marriage is so worthwhile.

I pass a lot of houses on my way home. Some pretty, some expensive, some inviting—but my heart always skips a beat when I turn down the road and see my house nestled against the hill. I guess I'm especially proud of the house and the way it looks because I drew the plans myself. It started out large enough for us. I even had a study—two teenage boys now reside in there. And it had a guest room—my girl and nine dolls are permanent guests. It had a small room Peg had hoped would be her sewing room—two boys swinging on the dutch door have claimed this room as their own. So it really doesn't look right now as if I'm much of an architect.

But it will get larger again. One by one they will go away: to work, to college, to service, to their own homes and then there will be room. A guest room, a study and a sewing room for just the two of us. But it won't be empty. Every corner, every room, every nick in the coffee table will be crowded with memories. Memories of picnics, parties, Christmases, bedside vigils, summers, fires, winters, going barefoot, leaving for vacation, black eyes, ball games, first dates, graduations, bicycles, dogs, boat rides, meals, rabbits and a thousand other things that fill the lives of those who would raise five. And Peg and I will sit quietly by the fire and listen to the laughter in the walls.[7]

I wish for you memories like this.

13.

UNLEASHING HOPE IN YOUR KIDS

I have no greater joy than to hear that my children walk in truth.

3 John 1:4 KJV

Children are more than we think they are; they can do more than we think they can do. All they need is a vote of confidence from grownups, whom they will ultimately replace anyway. Their dream today will become the realities of tomorrow.

Wess Stafford, former president and
CEO of Compassion International

Four expectant fathers were in a hospital waiting room while their wives were in labor. The nurse arrived and announced to the first man, "Congratulations, sir! You're the father of twins."

"What a coincidence!" the man said with obvious pride. "I work for the Minnesota Twins."

The nurse returned in a while and said to the second man, "You, sir, are the father of triplets."

"Wow! That's an incredible coincidence," he said. "I work for 3M."

An hour later, while the first two men were still passing cigars around, the nurse came back. She turned to the third man, who had been very quiet in the corner, and announced that his wife had just given birth to quadruplets. Stunned, he could not reply.

"I don't believe it," he stammered as he regained his composure. "I work for the Four Seasons Hotel."

After hearing this, everybody's attention turned to the fourth guy, who had just fainted, flat out on the floor. The nurse rushed to his side. After some time, he slowly gained consciousness. When he was finally able to speak, they could hear him whispering the same phrase over and over again: "I should have never taken that job at 7-11."[1]

Ask any parent, whether they have one kid or eleven, and they'll tell you the task of parenting can be a challenge. Ask anyone who works with teenagers, and they'll tell you it's not getting easier.

I taught adolescent development to graduate students and wrote a lot of books for teenagers and for those who work with them. I spent a ton of time with kids and teenagers, and I still do. I like it. A lot. So it's no surprise that author and youth leader Josh McDowell is a friend. Recently, he spoke at our Thrive Leadership Conference and surprised the crowd when he declared the number one fear of American parents today: parents fear that they will not be able to pass on their values, morals, or faith to their kids.

Just look at these sobering statistics about US teenagers:

- The US has the highest teen pregnancy and birthrate rate in the developed world.[2]
- Each year 400,000 teen girls give birth in the United States.[3]
- Every day 959 teenage girls get abortions.[4]
- The United States has the highest rate of STD infection in the industrialized world.[5]
- Every year one in four teens contracts an STD/STI.[6]
- Every year 4,600 youth commit suicide.[7]
- Every year 157,000 youth receive medical care for self-inflicted injuries.[8]

It is no exaggeration to say that young people are the greatest casualty of the sexual revolution:

- Every nineteen seconds a baby is born to an unmarried mother.

- Every eight seconds during the school year a public high school student drops out.
- Every forty-seven seconds a child is abused or neglected.
- Every three minutes a child is arrested for a drug offense.
- Every seven minutes a child is arrested for a violent offense.
- Every three hours and fifteen minutes a child or teen is killed by a firearm.
- Every six hours a child commits suicide.[9]

Statistics like these make you wonder if it is even possible to raise G-rated kids in an X-rated world. I believe the answer is no. (Just kidding!) I believe the answer is a resounding *yes*—provided that we make *one major shift* in how we parent kids. A graduate education on parenting is distilled in this next paragraph, so read carefully.

One Primary Shift: Turning Them On, Not Off

Parents provide both direction and motivation. Direction-based parenting tends to deliver guilt. Motivation-based parenting tends to deliver hope. As a parent, you have to *provide* direction, but ineffective parents *major* in delivering direction. That tends to be guilt-based, without motivation. Effective parents deliver *both* direction and motivation, which brings hope.

The single most profound thing ever penned on the subject of parenting is, "Children are a gift of the LORD. . . . Like arrows in the hand of a warrior, so are the children of one's youth" (Psalm 127:3–4 NASB). The writer teaches children are like arrows. You do three things with an arrow:

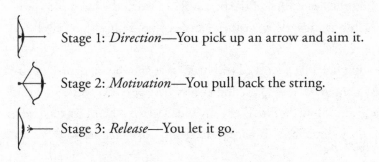

Stage 1: *Direction*—You pick up an arrow and aim it.

Stage 2: *Motivation*—You pull back the string.

Stage 3: *Release*—You let it go.

That image in those two verses summarizes the whole parenting task. You provide direction, you provide motivation, and you let the arrow fly. How do you build an environment so that on the day your kids go, they leave in the direction of your morals, your faith, and your values?

When kids are young, parenting is mostly about *direction*. As kids get to be teenagers, however, the job is much more challenging because it's now about motivation *and* direction. During this stage, most teenagers will go where they are motivated to go, not where they are directed to go. They no longer get out the manual and say, "What do Mommy and Daddy want me to do?" Instead, they wake up in the morning saying, "What do I feel like doing today?" and they go do that. Inner motivation has taken over.

Our problem as Christian parents is that we tend to be great at direction but not at motivation. Many of us place our kids in Christian schools or homeschool them so they can get even *more* direction. We haul them to church for even more direction. Then we struggle when our kids hit the teen years and a little rebellion starts up. Many parents respond by increasing the amount of direction (at increased amounts of volume), instead of supplying good motivation. That creates a culture of shame instead of a culture of hope. The problem is, *kids only flourish in a motivational culture of hope.*

We need to learn what turns them on, not off. On innumerable occasions, I've seen a well-meaning person do something that he or she thought would turn kids on, when in fact it turned them off, and the person had no clue. We mistakenly think that more information will provide more desire. It usually doesn't.

As kids grow older, we have to become much better at reaching the heart rather than filling the head. One of the best ways to reach the heart is to provide hope, to help our kids see what they can become, rather than dwell on what they are.

My whole adult life, I have worked with teenagers and their parents, speaking in churches, conferences, schools, and everywhere else. Everyone asks the exact same question: "How do I motivate my kids so that when I let them go, they go in a healthy direction?" Because I have only one chapter to write on motivation (and you may have only minutes before you'll need it), I'll give you a snapshot of what this looks like. Here are two barriers and three builders that will help every parent become more effective connecting with their kids and influencing them to become more productive and hope-filled.

Two Barriers and Three Builders

 Barrier #1: Do not delay joyful living until your kids turn eighteen and leave the house.

I have met countless parents whose parenting strategy *seems* to be, "My kids just turned thirteen. I am going to be on task, uptight, focused, and as miserable as I need to be for the next seven years . . . because I believe this will attract them to my faith and values."

Nobody—I mean *nobody*—is ever attracted to that kind of shame-based, tension-filled parenting. Most kids do much better if their parents are on their side, not on their back.

I want the number one sound in my house to be the sound of laughter. I want the strongest memories of my kids to be the vacations we took, not the lectures I delivered. Years from now, I want my kids still laughing about the time we threw Mom in the pool and (barely) lived to tell about it.

Your kids are attracted by the life you live, not the speeches you give.

 Barrier #2:
Don't let your teenagers intimidate you.

Sure, they're younger and probably thinner, they think they're cooler, and Hollywood tells them they're smarter. There's a difference, however, between *acting* sophisticated and *being* mature.

As sociologist Jean Potuchek said, "There are some cultures in which the elderly are revered for their experience and wisdom, but American society values youth and denigrates age. In this culture, the greatest compliment one can pay an older person is to tell them they seem or look younger than they are."[10] How dumb is all that?

I met a couple of parents who are the exact opposite. They picked me up at the airport the last time I spoke at a family conference in Seattle. We were driving through the ultrahip downtown area when the wife said, "Honey, this is the spot."

Her husband and I both said, "What spot?"

"Last week I was driving downtown with my sixteen-year-old 'too cool for life' daughter," she said. "At that stoplight, I glanced out the window, saw something, and yelled, 'Honey, *duck*!' I pushed my daughter's head down and sped two blocks down the street. She was saying, 'Mom, what is it? A carjacker, a gun, a robber?'

"Two blocks later, I took a deep breath and pulled back my hand. I said, 'Honey, I'm sorry. I saw one of my best friends and couldn't bear to be seen with my teenage daughter!'"

This mom played a prank on her daughter but also showed a great example of how not to be intimidated by a "too-cool-for-life" teen.

 Builder #1:
Stay future-focused.

I'm in a Wednesday morning men's Bible study with about twenty community and business leaders. One of them is a really sharp former police officer who is now a financial adviser controlling hundreds of millions of dollars. His daughter, also bright, is in college and works for him during the summer. He called her into his office one day, thinking one of those stern Dad conversations would give her a little motivation, and then proceeded to read her the riot act.

"I know you had a great year at college, but it's time to get serious and get focused. The job market is tough, so decide what you're going to do and buckle down. It's time to get after it."

The Wednesday before he did this, we had given everyone in the group a devotional, hoping to encourage the guys. He didn't read it until the morning after he talked with his daughter. He called me that afternoon.

"Ray," he said, "that devotional has changed everything."

"What happened?"

"I read this line: 'Hope is the greatest gift that any leader gives to his people.' And I realized I totally blew it yesterday. I gave my daughter everything except hope."

As soon as he realized his mistake, he said he called his daughter into his office a second time.

"Honey, I just want to tell you I'm sorry," he said. "You have an incredible future, and I'm committed to helping you find it. You're bright. You're smart. You're articulate. God has some great days ahead for you. It's gonna be fun to help you figure it out."

Then they talked, almost cried, laughed as peers, and left as friends. In just twenty-four hours, my friend's relationship with his daughter had changed completely.

His story got me thinking. What would happen in the lives of our kids if we started relating to them consistently on the basis of future hope? If my friend saw such a remarkable change in just twenty-four hours, what would happen if we brought future hope into the equation during all the years God gives us with our children? The discipline of asking "What can this person become?" is crucial to fueling hope and achieving dreams.

Here's another example, taken from chapter 21 of the gospel of John. It starts with the sun rising on Easter Sunday morning. Peter has had a rough couple of days. After bragging about his courage, he has denied Jesus three times, been intimidated by a little girl, lost his best friend and leader to a tortured death, and gone back to his former life. Could things get worse? They do.

Peter fishes all night and catches nothing. As he's reaching shore in the breaking dawn, he hears a familiar voice. It's Jesus. *He's back?* Given how the last forty-eight hours have been, Peter is trying to figure out if this is good news or bad news. He's thinking, *Am I going to be welcomed or banished? Am I going to been seen as a son or a sinner?*

During an amazing breakfast conversation, Jesus does two things with Peter. First, Jesus asks him three *present-tense* questions (*"Do you love Me?"* three times). Then Jesus gives him three *future-tense* assignments (*"Feed My sheep"* three times).

Not one time does Jesus bring up Peter's past.

In that one conversation, Jesus therapeutically freed Peter from his past, restored their relationship, and set Peter free for what was going to be a powerful future. Peter, starting from this track record of failure, goes on to become the first great leader of the early church.

How does this happen? Simple and profound. The main influencer in Peter's life stayed future-focused, even in times of failure. We talked about the most important question to ask, and it remains true, *especially* when somebody has let you down. The best question for staying future-focused about someone is not, "What is he or she like now?" The best question to raise the Hope Quotient in anybody of any age is, "What can he or she become?"

 Builder #2:
Believe that God can use kids and teenagers.

God can use kids. They're more capable than you think. The same Spirit who directs and energizes adult believers also directs and energizes kids and teenage believers. When we underestimate our kids, we rob *them* of hope and also diminish our own supplies.

Almost seventy years ago, a Philadelphia congregation watched three nine-year-old boys get baptized and join the church. As membership dwindled over the years, the church sold its building and disbanded. One of the boys baptized decades before was named Tony Campolo, who grew up to have a major impact on the evangelical church as a leader. Tony recalled,

> When I was doing research in the archives of our denominations, I decided to look up the church report for the year of my baptism. There was my name, and Dick White's. He's now a missionary. Bert Newman, now a professor of theology at an African seminary, was also there. Then I read the church report for "my" year: "It has not been a good year for our church. We have lost 27 members. Three joined, and they were only children."[11]

They were only children. Really? In November 2012, Tony Campolo received a Lifetime Achievement Award from the National Youth Worker's Convention. The award went to a man who, it said, "has defined and courageously pioneered what it means to encourage, care and lead students, possessing the qualities that inspire us and provoke us to continue the journey into the future with boldness and confidence. As a result of Tony's life of ministry and leadership he has left a legacy of encouragement and hope to youth workers and students everywhere."[12]

Never underestimate what the Holy Spirit will do in partnership with a child's life.

Builder #3:
Expose your kids to significant events and experiences.

Every spring break, Azusa Pacific University takes five thousand teens to northern Mexico to build homes, churches, orphanages, and medical clinics. Last year, I heard about two young women who went with them. I'll call them Amanda and Jessica. They worked the first day at a really tough village. Kids crawled on them for hours in a hot, windy town. After they finished, although they were tired, they said, "Let's stop at the house of that woman we met earlier today and pray with her!"

The girls searched out the woman's house. As they talked with her, Amanda looked down at the poor woman's feet, all bruised and cut up because her cheap sandals were disintegrating. Amanda thought she heard God whisper, *"Give her your shoes."* Amanda thought, *Uh, these are the only shoes I have.* She heard again, *"Give her your shoes."* She thought, *God, I'm going to be here for seven days, and this is only day one!* She heard again, *"Give her your shoes."* Amanda pulled off her shoes and handed them to the woman. As she did, Jessica pulled hers off and said, "You can have mine too."

Two exhausted but satisfied American teens picked their way back to camp barefoot—more confident, more mature, more hope-filled.

What develops unselfishness in today's teenagers? What produces values? What builds Christlike character? What creates a heart of compassion when their culture screams, "It's all about you"? How do we help teenagers hear from God and stretch their imaginations of what they can become and the impact they can have? All of that develops when we expose kids to experiences that have enough octane to captivate their hearts and minds.

I pulled my own kids out of school at pretty regular intervals to have experiences like these. I pulled them out every year for our Thrive Leadership Conference because I wanted them to see four thousand adults from around the world listening, learning, and laughing together. I took my daughters to Africa and Europe for six weeks to meet some world-changing, poverty-impacting leaders. I sometimes pulled my kids out of school for church staff retreats because I wanted them to hang out for forty-eight hours with some of the most fun ministry-minded leaders on the planet. I took my kids to visit colleges and universities to show them that high school would not last forever, so why wreck your life to please a bunch of people you'll never see again? I believe in education, twenty-one years of it and growing. I just tried to make sure that my kids' education was not confined to the four walls of a classroom.

Let's learn to turn our kids on, not off. Let's give them both direction *and* motivation. And when it's time to let the arrows fly, let's trust that the hope we instilled in them will help them fly straight and true.

Cultivate Close Connections

Nothing raises children's confidence and self-esteem like an adult who believes that the God who made them will actually use them. This breaks a negative self-image cycle and replaces it with a far more hope-filled cycle of positive self-esteem. Here's a diagram that shows how these cycles work:

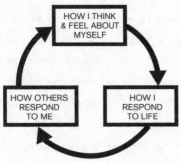

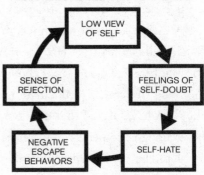

Parents have a unique ability and special power to connect with the teens under their own roof, but other adults with a heart for kids and a flair for the creative can also have a profound effect and give birth to hope. Never underestimate the power of a connected adult. I heard a Young Life leader say, "Any kid will do great if you give them two things: a warm welcome and an adult who's crazy about them."

Bill's story.

Years ago, I teamed up with a man named Bill to work with some teenagers. Bill never taught or preached. In fact, he never did *anything* up front. But I saw him care for a group of seventh-grade boys in an astonishing way. A lot of them had no dads, and others came from dysfunctional homes, yet they were developing qualities I didn't think they could even imagine. Finally one day I talked to Bill.

"You are unbelievable with kids," I said. "What's your secret to transforming these junior high boys?"

"I don't have a secret."

"Come on, man! What are you doing with these kids?"

"Nothing that everybody else isn't doing."

I kept after him. Finally he said, "Well, if there *is* anything I'm doing, it would be this notebook."

I thought, *I don't know what's in that notebook, but let's publish it and I'll pay off my college loans! We'll sell it to everybody who works with junior high kids!*

"What is it?" I asked.

He acted embarrassed as he pulled out a beat-up, but pretty standard skinny spiral notebook.

"Here," he said. "I've never showed it to anybody."

I opened the front cover and at the top of the first page, I read the name of a junior high kid, saw his picture, and below it a description of the boy's family situation. Underneath that, I read five or six things that Bill had been praying for. I flipped to the next page, saw the name of another kid, another picture, another situation, another list Bill was praying about. Third page, fourth page, fifth page, same thing—eleven pages in all, featuring eleven different junior high boys.

"Every morning when I read my Bible," Bill said, "I look at these kids and pray for each one of them. I usually connect with them during the week to see how it's going."

Those kids have never recovered from Bill's influence. Despite some horrendous home situations, Bill helped to raise their sights on what they could become.

Ray's story.

I realized early on that I had a bank account with each of my four kids that had nothing to do with money. It was an *emotional* bank account. When I spent time with them, laughed together, went out on daddy-daughter date nights, took my boys to restaurants every other week to talk about what *they* wanted to talk about, it put "money" in their emotional accounts.

When we had to have a tough conversation, when discipline was needed, when correction was given, when I sometimes blew it, these amounted to a withdrawal. The withdrawals needed to be balanced with emotional deposits—words and actions of love and affirmation. Parents and their kids end up in trouble and turmoil when we make more withdrawals than deposits.

To this day, I ask myself about once a month how emotionally connected I am to each of my family members. Whatever I discover, I try to take action on. This has major benefits, not just for affecting and influencing the direction of their lives. Over time, it provides the relationships everyone hopes for.

While writing this chapter, I'm recovering from a shoulder surgery I had two days ago because of a disagreement with a jet ski. (It won.) Three hours ago, my twin daughters walked into my bedroom and said, "Surprise! We wanted to come home and see if you were okay." They drove eight hours from college today just to check on their dad. I just learned that daughters are the best pain medication a parent could ever need.

It is never too late to begin building these kinds of connections with the people you love. Here's an example of a guy who did it better than all of us.

The Coolest Dad's story.

Angie calls her dad the "Coolest Dad in the Universe." She wrote:

He was 50 years old when I was born, and a "Mr. Mom" long before anyone had a name for it. I didn't know why he was home instead of Mom, but I was young and the only one of my friends who had their dad around. I considered myself very lucky.

Dad did so many things for me during my grade school years. . . . He always had my lunch ready for me when I came home. . . .

In high school and no longer able to go home for lunch, I began taking my own. Dad would get up a little early and make it for me. I never knew what to expect. The outside of the sack might be covered with his rendering of a mountain scene (it became his trademark) or a heart inscribed with "Dad-n-Angie K.K." in its center. Inside there would be a napkin with that same heart or an "I love you." . . .

I used to hide my lunch so no one would see the bag or read the napkin, but that didn't last long. One of my friends saw the napkin one day, grabbed it, and passed it around the lunch room. My face burned with embarrassment. To my astonishment, the next day all my friends were waiting to see the napkin. From the way they acted, I think they all wished they had someone who showed them that kind of love. I was so proud to have him as my father. . . .

And still it didn't end. When I left home for college (the last one to leave), I thought the messages would stop. But my friends and I were glad that his gestures continued.

I missed seeing my dad every day after school and so I called him a lot. My phone bills got to be pretty high. It didn't matter what we said; I just wanted to hear his voice. We started a ritual during that first year that stayed with us. After I said good-bye he always said, "Angie?"

"Yes, Dad?" I'd reply.

"I love you."

"I love you, too, Dad."

I began getting letters almost every Friday. . . . Many times the envelopes were addressed in crayon, and along with the enclosed letters were usually drawings of our cat and dog, stick figures of him and Mom, and if I had been home the weekend before, of me racing around town with friends and using the house as a pit stop. He also had his mountain scene and the heart-encased inscription, Dad-n-Angie K.K.

The mail was delivered every day right before lunch, so I'd have his letters with me when I went to the cafeteria. I realized it was useless to hide them because my roommate was a high school friend who knew about his napkins. Soon it became a Friday afternoon ritual. I would read the letters, and the drawing and envelope would be passed around.

It was during this time that Dad became stricken with cancer. When the letters didn't come on Friday, I knew that he had been sick and wasn't able to write. He used to get up at 4:00 A.M. so he could sit in the quiet house and do his letters. If he missed his Friday delivery, the letters would usually come a day or two later. But they always came. My friends used to call him "Coolest Dad in the Universe." And one day they sent him a card bestowing that title, signed by all of them. I believe he taught all of us about a father's love. . . .

Throughout my four years of college, the letters and phone calls came at regular intervals. But then the time came when I decided to come home and be with him because he was growing sicker, and I knew that our time together was limited. . . . In the end he didn't recognize who I was and would call me the name of a relative he hadn't seen in many years. Even though I knew it was due to his illness, it still hurt that he couldn't remember my name.

I was alone with him in his hospital room a couple of days before he died. We held hands and watched TV. As I was getting ready to leave, he said, "Angie?"

"Yes, Dad?"

"I love you."

"I love you, too, Dad."[13]

Whatever the age of your kids (or grandchildren) it is never too late to become the number one encourager in their lives. It will make all the difference for them—and you!

14.

UNLEASHING HOPE IN YOUR CAREER

Sow your seed in the morning,
and at evening let not your hands be idle,
for you do not know which will succeed,
whether this or that,
or whether both will do equally well.

ECCLESIASTES 11:6

Whatever luck I had, I made. I paid my dues in sweat and
concentration.

CHUCK NORRIS

Carol and I lounged around a pool that overlooked a crystal ocean framed by a stunning landscape as we celebrated our thirtieth wedding anniversary at the Montage Laguna Beach Resort. Generous friends provided an unbelievable room at this five-star, world-class resort. God provided outstanding weather. An exceptional hotel staff provided the rest.

Everywhere we turned, friendly, fun, helpful, motivated, bright, energetic people were willing to help. The staff worked as a team, treating not just the guests with class but also each other. They consistently went the extra mile in everything they did. It made for such an amazing atmosphere that I began talking to some of the employees and senior managers. Over and over, I heard the same story. One manager explained the whole thing.

"Most workplaces try to hire people who will do a great job," she said. "It's somewhat easy to find people who will do a good job. At this hotel, we try to hire, train, celebrate, reward, and promote people who do a good job and also *set great culture and atmosphere.* The staff love being here as much as the guests and don't want to leave. No one wants to walk out of a situation where the atmosphere is positive, gracious, fun, and motivating."

In other words this hotel looked for people with sky-high HQ.

Everyone does.

Every church, company, school, team, or five-star resort is trying to find, train, and keep these kinds of people. Yet the workplace is the *last* place we find culture like this. Churches are no exception. So the question becomes, "If you are currently not finding hope *at* your work, then how can you bring hope *into* your work?" In other words . . .

- How do you set a culture of hope at your place of business?
- How do you elevate the atmosphere and so, perhaps, raise the HQ of your entire office, department, division, warehouse, or company?
- What can you do to help raise the culture of hope in your workplace?

I'm going to give you five ways to *raise hope* where you are right now. Then I'll give you four questions I'd like you to ask yourself, to see if you should *stay* where you are right now.

Five Ways to Raise Hope Where You Are Now

No matter what the atmosphere and culture of your current workplace may be, there are five ways you can raise the hope level where you are now.

1. Arrive with energy.

Five days a week, Harold Fisher worked as an award-winning architect at the Michigan firm he founded. He specialized in church architecture and designed more than five hundred church buildings for fifty different religious organizations. To keep himself fit, Harold worked out at a gym twice a week and did yoga.

Nothing too remarkable about that, right? What if I told you that I just described Harold Fisher a month *after* his hundredth birthday? In 2001, a national nonprofit organization honored Harold as "America's Oldest Worker." When someone asked him how it felt to get such an honor at his age, he replied, "I just kept on living. I love my work, I love designing. It's kept me alive."

Harold told the interviewer he's still learning new things on the job, and every morning he wakes up with new ideas. "Designing is thrilling to me and I have designs running through my head all the time," he said. "I don't think of it as work."[1]

Harold embodies one of the keys to bringing hope into the workplace. *Every day, he arrived with energy.* When he used words like "love" and "thrilled" to describe his work, he unintentionally explained his strategy for chasing despair out of his office.

When I look for new employees, I intentionally look for energy. Hey, I can get people *without* energy for *free*!

I'm on the board of Azusa Pacific University. Three of my kids currently attend there. That means a lot of my time—and almost *all* of my money—are spent in Azusa, California. The most popular person in the town, believe it or not, is the mayor, Joe Rocha. Joe is a young—midsixties—father and grandfather who has been the mayor since 2007.

Last year, I was with five thousand people welcoming incoming students at APU's Felix Event Center when they introduced the mayor. He stunned everybody by saying, "Welcome to Azusa. I am now your mayor, and as long as you live in my town, I'm here to serve you. I am available for whatever you need. You're in my city now, which means you are now part of my family, so I want to give you my personal cell phone number. If you ever need *anything*, give me a call."

Joe Rocha is reelected by a landslide every time. People who arrive with energy are always in demand.

▮ 2. Live and lead with passion.

Bringing passion to your job changes the work landscape. Passion brings life; apathy deadens. When you arrive with passion, you can take advantage of the opportunities disguised as *hard work*. I'd much rather have to ask someone to tone things down than to amp them up.

I love working with our worship leader, Lincoln Brewster. Besides being a fantastic husband, father, and friend, his guitar skills are simply amazing. No wonder he played guitar with Steve Perry of Journey when he was just nineteen. When Lincoln arrived to become the worship leader at our church, he was so sensitive about people perceiving worship as performance that he became a pretty tame version of himself.

That all changed at Easter of his second year. Lincoln does this great guitar riff in his song "Let the Praises Ring." So, as we were coming into our eighth and last Easter service, I met Lincoln and another great guitarist, Brandon, behind the platform.

"Guys, this is *Easter*. Christ is *risen*!" They just nodded at me. I could tell they still didn't realize I was tired of Lawrence Welk, so I drove it home. "Listen. This is the *greatest* celebration of the *greatest* victory ever won. If there was ever a time to blow the roof off the church, if there was ever a day worth that kind of passion and celebration, it's *Easter*! So let people cut loose and *celebrate* the resurrection! Those guitars are no more or less spiritual than an organ or a trumpet, so pick them up and *tear the house down*! If anybody complains, I'll take the heat."

The next service, they got to the right song, hopped down on the bottom stage, and squared off. Those guitars just screamed, alternating back and forth. The place exploded with praise! Energy! Passion! Worship filled the auditorium and people celebrated the resurrection like few services I've ever experienced. Something broke loose that day in our worship, and it's never been the same since.

"I put them up to that," I told our people after the music ended. "So send *me* the letters."

The presence of passion changes things. It blasts open creaky doors, breaks apart rusty chains, floods darkened rooms with light, and chases away gloom with laughter and joy. In other words, *it sets culture*.

3. Stay positive under pressure.

Atmosphere and culture are either developed or destroyed by how people respond when times get tough. It's been said, "People are like teabags—if you want to find out what's inside them, drop them into hot water." What comes out when the heat is turned up often shapes the environment more than any other factor.

The secret to much of success in anything is learning how to perform well under pressure. Or, as I'm constantly saying to my kids, no matter what happens, keep your cool!

A young man raised by a single mother learned the same lessons under a different kind of pressure. Chuck was so shy in school that he couldn't stand up to do a book report, taking the F rather than facing his classmates. After enlisting in the air force, he became intrigued by the martial arts, earning black belts in more than one discipline.

Once discharged, he couldn't find people to spar with. He decided he would have to teach people martial arts. The first time he tried to make a public announcement about starting a school, he was so nervous, he has no memory of it to this day. He ended up the first person from the Western Hemisphere to win a karate world championship, then broke more records by defending it for six consecutive years.

Chuck's fledgling martial arts school in Southern California caught the eye of Hollywood actors and producers. Soon he found himself urged into acting by one of his students, actor Steve McQueen. Chuck was cast in bit parts with Hollywood luminaries such as Dean Martin and John Wayne. After his starring role opposite Bruce Lee in *Return of the Dragon*, Chuck Norris became a household name.

After the films were produced, Chuck had to promote them, forcing him to face the public on a daily basis. He learned how to face his fears and calm his nerves. "I've always found that anything worth achieving will always have obstacles, and you've got to have that drive and determination to overcome those obstacles, route to whatever it is that you want to accomplish," he says.

Chuck's action movies became huge hits. He furthered his career with the television series *Walker, Texas Ranger*, well known for its family values and for its longevity. You cannot flip channels without seeing it somewhere. (We'll probably one day see reruns even in heaven.) Not to mention, he's a great Christian and a great sport, the target of probably the most jokes on the Internet. My favorite is that when Chuck Norris does push-ups, he pushes the world down.

In his career, Chuck has had to learn the hard way to stay positive under pressure. "A lot of times people look at the negative side of what they feel they can't do," he states. "I always look at the positive side of what I can do."[2]

4. Be a peacemaker, not a troublemaker.

Several years ago, we had a talented, gifted, bright, driven, motivated person on our staff . . . whom we had to lay off. The way the supervisor put it, "Whenever that person does a job it is done well, but there is so much relational broken glass, it simply isn't worth it."

You know who that guy is. You've worked around that woman. They may be talented and brilliant, but their IQ is not matched by their HQ.

Some people are like porcupines. They have a lot of fine points. They're just hard to get close to. Some people love to argue. Some people are easily offended. With some people, you have to walk on eggshells because they are always getting their feelings hurt. Some people are defensive. Some people are always intentionally or unintentionally hurting other people.

This is not to say everything is going to be smooth sailing. One of the things I appreciate about the Bible is that the writers of Scripture were so honest about this. James and John had a sibling rivalry. Paul and Barnabas's personnel disagreement led to them parting ways. Paul confronted Peter in the book of Acts.

Relational tension is going to happen. Just don't be the glass-breaker. Be the relationship-maker.

5. Add value.

My cell phone lit up one day with a call from a "private" number, and my curiosity led me to answer it. Glad I did; it was John Maxwell.

"Ray!" John said. "What are you doing next Tuesday?"

"Why?"

"I am playing golf in LA and want you to be my guest."

"Coincidentally, John, my Tuesday schedule just cleared!"

For an entire day, John asked questions about me, my world, my leadership, my future plans. No sermon. No leadership lessons. Just a lot of laughing, a great connection, and a guy in a golf cart adding value to my life.

People who add value to your life are a great gift. Hope rises. Vision rises. Confidence rises. Imagine the impact on a company, church, team, or family if everybody arrived with one purpose—to add value to every other person in the room.

Ask Yourself Some Smart Questions

Before they take a job, most people ask a lot of questions about the company. The problem is those are the *only* questions they ask. They seldom ask questions they need to know about *themselves*. You'll do a lot better at bringing hope into your place of business when you answer four critical questions about yourself.

If you want to maximize your impact . . . if you want to make sure what you do is fulfilling . . . if you want to be at your best day after day, the following four questions are critical.

Question 1: What are my unique factors?

Consider your personal strengths and abilities:

- What are you really great at?
- What can you be the best in the world at?
- What have others told you that you do really, really well?

There's a reason I don't lead worship. There's a reason I'm not trying to play professional basketball (anymore). There's a reason I'm not living on a fishing boat. What it takes to do those things are not my strengths and abilities.

People who take the time to figure out what they do best, and do it, not only like going to work—they feel better at work, are paid better because of their work, and generally arrive home in a better mood. One of the keys to life is to figure out what God made you to do better than most people and *run as fast as you can in that direction.*

Question 2: When am I most fulfilled?

It is possible to build a life with a lot of *success* but very little *significance.* Ultimately, that's not going to lead to any sense of personal fulfillment. Imagine your life as a movie. Skip to the end and play the conclusion. Thirty or forty years from now, what do you want to have accomplished? What do you want to see at the end of your life's movie?

To help us get perspective, my wife and I ask a question before undertaking any major project: "What are we going to be glad we did twenty-five thousand years from now?" In other words, twenty-five thousand years after we've been in heaven, how are we going to be glad to have lived?

Four out of my five last career moves have resulted in a drop in salary. Carol and I made the move because we asked, "Will this move help us have greater impact than if we stay?" If it had greater impact, we made the move and sorted out the consequences.

I'm not advocating you figure out how to make less money. That is usually pretty easy and doesn't take much thought. I'm advocating that there is a world of causes out there, and you have only one life to make an impact. Find out what you're great at. Use those gifts to make the largest impact you can for God and for good.

Question 3: When am I happiest?

This is a more important question than most people realize, because happiness and fulfillment have to be balanced. Spending the rest of my life playing golf every day with my three best friends would make me happy, but it's probably not going to be fulfilling. On the other hand, if I'm not doing things I like to do and I'm grinding life out only on the things that bring fulfillment, I'll probably be miserable doing it and end up quitting. Impact and fulfillment happen best when both are occurring. So ask yourself:

- What fires you up?
- What do you absolutely love to do?
- On days when you're glad about going to work, what are you doing?
- What gives you the greatest pleasure?
- What makes you smile?

Conversely:

- What makes you unhappy?
- Every job has a "pay the rent" un-fun part, but what kind of work tends to lift your spirits?

Question 4: What is best for my family?

There is little joy in the lives of people who have sacrificed their families in order to pursue some career goal. As you think through the first three questions, how could your answers dovetail with your answer to this fourth question? What would make both you and your family happy?

After our son Mark was born, we moved from California to Chicago. Then we had Scott. Then Carol contracted pregnancy again. I got home one day and she handed me some Doublemint chewing gum, and that's how I found out we were expecting twin daughters. A year later, we were sitting in the living room with four little kids crawling all over the floor. Carol isn't usually wistful, but that day she said, "I wish our kids could know my parents better, and they aren't getting any younger."

I couldn't shake her offhanded comment. I'm not wired to think these ways, and I had three really important jobs at the time with a lot of responsibility, so it didn't make sense to leave Chicago. But her parents were in Southern California and her dad had already turned seventy. I started praying about it and felt like God was speaking to my heart. I thought, *If you don't make this happen and her dad passes away without your kids ever knowing him, Carol will have to carry that for the rest of her life.* Then I thought, *What if, years down the road, Carol woke up one day and said, "All we've ever done is what Ray wanted to do"?*

I found a new job and we moved back to California in September. Four months later, I was the last one to wake up on an early Christmas morning. I started down the stairs to join them, but for some reason I stopped on the landing and just stood there looking. Below me in the living room was one of the coolest sights I've ever seen.

Sitting on the big old couch in front of the Christmas tree was Carol's dad. All four little grandkids in their pajamas were crawling all over him and the five of them were cracking up laughing. I stood there and watched them for a long time, completely choked up and so grateful to God for grabbing my attention with Carol's comment. I thought, *God, thank You. It worked.* We had seven great years with Grandpa before he passed away, and our kids will have a lifetime of memories. So will my wife. So will I.

It didn't make sense, but it did. You might have to make some moves, too, in order to unleash hope.

15.

UNLEASHING HOPE IN YOUR CHURCH

All the believers were together and had everything in common. . . . Every day they continued to meet together. . . . They broke bread in their homes and ate together with glad and sincere hearts, praising God and enjoying the favor of all the people.

ACTS 2:44–47

Jesus promised His disciples three things—that they would be completely fearless, absurdly happy and in constant trouble.

G. K. CHESTERTON

My friend Dave Olson wrote a great book, *The American Church in Crisis*. A quick survey of the facts reveals the following:

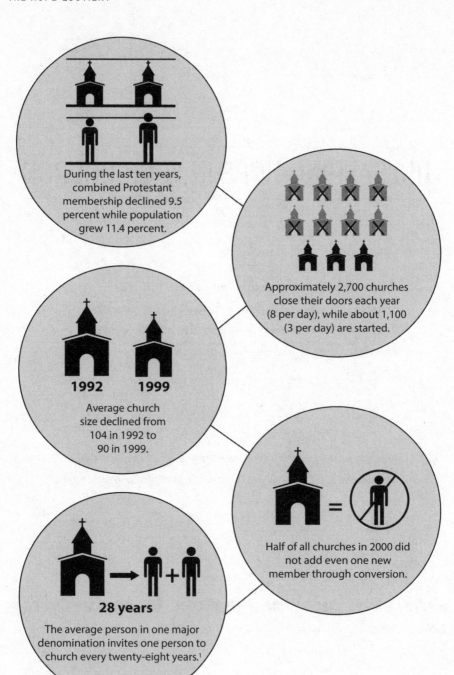

During the last ten years, combined Protestant membership declined 9.5 percent while population grew 11.4 percent.

Approximately 2,700 churches close their doors each year (8 per day), while about 1,100 (3 per day) are started.

1992 1999

Average church size declined from 104 in 1992 to 90 in 1999.

Half of all churches in 2000 did not add even one new member through conversion.

28 years

The average person in one major denomination invites one person to church every twenty-eight years.[1]

The church is the greatest institution ever created on earth, and it is the only thing Jesus ever promised to build. What went wrong?

Philip Yancey, in his outstanding book *What's So Amazing About Grace?* told a gripping story he heard from a friend who worked with the down-and-out in Chicago. His friend said,

> A prostitute came to me in wretched straits, homeless, sick, unable to buy food for her two-year-old daughter. Through sobs and tears, she told me she had been renting out her daughter—two years old!—to men interested in kinky sex. . . . She had to do it, she said, to support her own drug habit. I could hardly bear hearing her sordid story. For one thing, it made me legally liable—I'm required to report cases of child abuse. I had no idea what to say to this woman.
>
> At last I asked if she had ever thought of going to a church for help. I will never forget the look of pure, naïve shock that crossed her face. "Church!" she cried. "Why would I ever go there? I was already feeling terrible about myself. They'd just make me feel worse."[2]

People like this prostitute—people who needed forgiveness, grace, hope—run from today's church, and in record numbers.

The experience of the early Christians in the book of Acts was just the opposite. A scan of the hope-fueled, life-changing faith of the early Christians reveals that in New Testament times, people who needed hope looked to Jesus, and as a result . . .

The church exploded! Starting in Jerusalem, hope-filled, vibrant Christ-followers brought the love of Christ to the entire known world of their day.

Barriers were shattered! Empowered Christians broke racial, cultural, and ethnic barriers that had divided and held people captive for centuries.

Compassion was unleashed! Saturated in grace, early Christians brought help and hope to the poor (without any tax deductions promised!).

Lives, communities, cities, and countries were transformed by the love of Christ! This was a Christian church fueled by faith, hope, and love. When the world can run to that kind of church, marriages are helped and healed; lost people's lives and eternal destinies are changed; the poor are lifted; racial barriers are blown away; children, teens, singles, married people all find a family to belong to; and Christians discover the thrill of being used by God to change the world.

In other words, when the church is focused on Christ and fueled by hope, it is the most powerful force in the world.

Five characteristics marked those hope-filled early Christians. To the degree that we get these five things back into our churches today, we will again see the kinds of things happen in our churches that happened in the early church. It worked once—it *can* happen again!

Characteristic #1—Hope-Fueled Churches Believe God Has Better Days Ahead

I love consulting with pastors and churches from around the world through my work with Thriving Churches International. Almost without exception, when we walk into one of these environments, the starting point for all future health and growth for them is to begin to believe that God has better days ahead for them.

A church in our area called one day and said, "Can you guys get over here?" The sudden departure of their pastor under less-than-ideal circumstances meant the church was in crisis.

As I stood up that Sunday morning to speak to the congregation, you could have cut the tension with a knife. I walked up front, scanned this great group of people, many in tears, and said, "I want to let you know two things. Number one, I am sorry for what happened to your church.

"I have a second thing I want to say to you, and here it is: *I believe that God has better days ahead for you and your church.*"

It would be hard to describe the emotions that welled up in the congregation at that point. I heard some people crying, others applauding, and all of us felt a wave of hope rise in the room, probably for the first time in a very long time.

When hope rises in the heart of a church, Christ's followers get set free to dream and to believe that God has better days ahead. Hope raises the energy level of the congregation, and the people become far more positive. They start to say, "You know, this really could happen. Our best days really could be ahead!"

Our pastors from Bayside did all the preaching in that church for a year and a half, and during that time the congregation hired a great new pastor. Now they're off and running. I visited their leaders about a month ago, and they told me, "It's back, and it's better than ever!"

When a church and its people begin believing that God actually does have better days ahead, everything changes.

Characteristic #2—Hope-Fueled Churches Take God-Honoring Risks

Our churches struggle today because we've developed a watered-down version of the Christian faith that looks nothing like the vibrant, life-changing, world-impacting, risk-taking faith of the early church. How did *their* faith unleash hope?

- They were not afraid to take risks.
- They were not afraid to give sacrificially.
- They were not afraid to share their faith.
- They were not afraid to try new things.

What a contrast! Far too much of the American church is a risk-averse, self-centered, inward-focused, nothing-changes-here organization. The contrast couldn't be more dramatic. The main difference between these early believers and us is that they had a confident, risk-taking faith, and too often we don't.

About five years ago, our church got a call from a church in real trouble. It had enjoyed a big growth spurt under the leadership of its senior pastor, who spearheaded an effort to build a seven-hundred-seat auditorium. The church took out a loan in excess of $3 million . . . and then the pastor left to go elsewhere. The church went into rapid decline. They called, and I agreed to meet with their demoralized leadership team.

"We're getting foreclosed on," the leader said, laying out the financial reports. "We're down to one hundred eighty people. We're in debt. It's a mess!"

"Here's what I'll do," I said. "I'll meet with our board and ask if they'll accept the following plan. We will invite your members to worship at Bayside for four weeks. We'll have a prayer meeting after each service for anyone who wants to pray for your church. After a month, we'll help you relaunch."

I went back to our board for what I knew was going to be an unbelievable conversation.

"I met with this troubled church and I think we could have a positive impact on their church and community," I told them. "I recommend that we as a church back their $3.8 million loan. We're already stretched financially, and that's going to tap any ability for us to borrow for future growth. It's a huge risk to assume we can find a pastor willing to lead them. And, if this plan works and this church is revitalized, we're going to lose people and money."

"So, that's what we're voting on tonight," I said with a laugh.

"What happens if we get hurt financially and have to borrow?" one of our board members asked—obviously the most responsible person in the room. It was a legitimate question. He said, "We'll have no capacity to borrow because we'll have committed it all to this sinking ship."

"That's the risk," I said. With that, we voted.

We shut down that church for four weeks, then thrilled their banker (and scared ours) when we backed their loan. A month later, I preached at a reopening service and five hundred fifty people showed up. It was a blast. The place looked packed. Hope rose. We helped the church find a great senior pastor. They grew. Hope grew. Three years later, they took over the loan again (our banker was thrilled). Then they bought the property next door. Now they run over one thousand in weekly attendance, filling that auditorium twice every Sunday morning. They are changing their community and meeting more needs than ever before.

A hope-fueled church took a God-honoring risk that resulted in another church recovering from a meltdown, growing, and serving a beautiful community filled with people who need Jesus. Sometimes to walk on water you have to climb out of the boat.

Characteristic #3—Hope-Fueled Churches Unleash Compassion

The impact of our church was turned upside down six years ago because of a Bible study in Newport Beach, California. I'd flown down to meet with a group of leaders to talk about the subject of why churches were so disconnected from their communities. To be blunt about it, you could close the doors of the average church in America and the community would never miss it, because they have so little connection to the community. We studied the early church's pattern for affecting its community and I realized that, like almost every other church in America, our church had this all wrong.

Acts 2

"Selling their possessions and goods, they gave to anyone as he had need." (v. 45)	Good *Deeds*
"Every day they continued to meet together in the temple courts. They broke bread in their homes and ate together with glad and sincere hearts . . ." (v. 46)	Good *Will*
" . . . praising God and enjoying the favor of all the people. And the Lord added to their number daily those who were being saved." (v. 47)	Good *News*

The early church's pattern for impacting its community could not have been clearer. First, they started with *good deeds*. Selling their possessions and goods, they gave to anyone who had needs. That was their starting point. Those good deeds then led to *good will*: they had favor with God and with all the people. That is something the American church doesn't have and hasn't had for a while. In our study, we were shocked to comprehend these words. Their good deeds led to good will, and the very next verse reads, "And the Lord added to their number daily those who were being saved." That's *good news*. The early church's pattern was that *good deeds led to good will, which led to openness to the good news*.

I realized that, like many pastors of American churches, I had reversed this pattern at Bayside. We had been trying to deliver the good news without good deeds. No wonder there was no good will. I got home, called the staff together, and said, "This is going to mess up our church in some very good ways. We're switching things up because I believe the early church majored in unleashing compassion, and we have to pursue that pattern."

That one meeting changed everything. We began doing all kinds of things that we had never done before, like

- running special-needs kids' camps,
- collecting food and clothing donations every weekend to take to area shelters,
- finding people jobs through career ministry, and
- asking every family in our church to sponsor a child with Compassion International (now at seven thousand kids sponsored and growing each year).

The toughest thing of all to pull off, though, is Serve Weekend. Once a year, every year, we shut down our entire church for the weekend. We interview every principal and every mayor of the surrounding towns and choose projects by asking them, "What needs do you have that we could meet? We're not here to preach; we're here to serve."

Experts told us that if we didn't take an offering, we'd lose 1/52 of our income. And if we didn't open the church doors, people wouldn't serve anyway and we'd lose them to other churches.

We ignored the experts and hung up a sign in front of our facility that first Serve Weekend that said, "The church has left the building." Ten thousand people signed up *and* showed up. Serve Weekend changed our relationship with the community, with medical clinics downtown, with schools of every kind (I'll tell you a great story about that later), and more. And, despite the predictions of experts, our folks stepped up and met our church's needs.

Both our staff and our people made connections with individuals throughout the community that otherwise we likely never would have made. That weekend, barriers came down, and they continue to come down, because hope-fueled churches unleash compassion.

Characteristic #4—Hope-Fueled Churches Are Known by What They're For, Not What They're Against

An old joke represents for me the very kind of thing that the church needs to abandon if it is to change the perception of Christians. The joke goes like this:

Walking through a city late one night, I came upon a guy about to jump off a bridge. I said, "Wait a minute! Don't you believe in God?"

"Yeah," he said, "I do believe in God."

"Really? Are you a Christian or a Jew?"

"I'm a Christian."

"Me, too! Protestant or Catholic?"

"Protestant," answered the guy as he peered at the dark water far below.

"What denomination?"

"Baptist."

"Me, too. Northern or Southern?"

"Northern."

"Me, too. Northern Conservative Baptist or Northern Liberal Baptist?"

"Northern Conservative Baptist."

"Me, too! Are you Northern Conservative Reformed Baptist or Northern Conservative Fundamentalist Baptist?"

"Northern Conservative Fundamentalist Baptist."

"Me, too! This is incredible. Are you from the Northern Conservative

Fundamentalist Baptist Great Lakes Region, or the Northern Conservative Fundamentalist Baptist Eastern Region?"

"Northern Conservative Fundamentalist Baptist Great Lakes Region."

"Wow, me, too! Are you from the Northern Conservative Fundamentalist Baptist Great Lakes Region Council of 1879, or are you from the Northern Conservative Fundamentalist Baptist Great Lakes Region Council of 1912?"

"Northern Conservative Fundamentalist Baptist Great Lakes Region Council of 1912."

I said, "Die, heretic!" and pushed him off the bridge.[3]

Hope-based Christians realize that revival comes not when people become more religious but when religious people become more like *Christ*.

Characteristic #5—Hope-Fueled Churches Believe That Resurrection Works Best in Cemeteries

It's Easter Sunday morning. Christ is *alive*—and the disciples are a *mess*. Christ is *alive*? They have no clue. They walk into a room filled with anxiety and fear. Something happens in that room, and they walk out confident. They walk into a room filled with doubt and regret. They walk out filled with faith. They walk into a room crushed by discouragement. They walk out filled with hope. They had become a band of whimpering, fear-filled cowards, huddled in a room, having a gigantic pity party—but something happened in that room that changed *everything*.

- One minute they were defeated, the next they were dynamic.
- One minute they were afraid, the next they were courageous.
- One minute they were crushed, the next they exploded with power and changed human history.

What in the world did they discover in that room?
The angel put it this way, "He is not here. He is risen" (Matthew 28:6,

author's paraphrase). The early church believed *He is risen* were the three most important words in the Bible. Today a billion people gather to celebrate these words every weekend. *He is risen* separates Jesus from every other religion in history. *He is risen* made the Bible the best-selling book, parchment, or goatskin of all time. Those three words are the reason the Christian church believes that God raised His Son. Those three words are the reason the Christian church believes that all the hope you will ever need is available.

If God can raise His Son, that same power that defeated death can give you the power to live. It can raise a dead marriage. It can raise a dead career. It can raise a dead dream. It's the power to let go of guilt. It's the power to begin again. It's the power to bounce back from a broken heart. It's the power to become what you were always meant to be in the first place.

I saw it in action last week. Our staff meetings are generally a time when 188 team members celebrate with a party, but last week we had the most emotional moment we've ever shared. One of the staff, a retired pastor named Alan, walked into the room as we were starting. Three weeks ago, we mourned the passing of his wife. Now, he walked back into staff meeting for the first time, and the room erupted in a standing ovation. Then Alan said this: "I had the privilege of being married for fifty-one years to my best friend, the most beautiful woman in the world for me. Two weeks ago, she moved out and changed addresses. Someday in the future, I'll change addresses, too, and the next time we are together we will both be more alive than we have ever been."

He is risen are the three words that give the Christian church the solid foundation of hope to offer to every person on the planet. Those three words signal that death is defeated—for you, for me, for *everyone*. Those three words let you know that *anything is possible*. Those three words give us our hope, and there is no situation and no person that cannot be fueled by hope. And resurrection always works best in cemeteries.

16.

UNLEASHING HOPE IN YOUR COMMUNITY

Inasmuch as you did it to one of the least of these My brethren, you did it to Me.

MATTHEW 25:40 NKJV

Twenty years from now you will be more disappointed by the things that you didn't do than by the ones you did do. Sail away from the safe harbor.

MARK TWAIN

One of my closest friends in the world just died. I heard the news of his fatal heart attack as I started writing this chapter. Sherwood Carthen was just fifty-four years old, but already he had accomplished far more for our city than most leaders do in a lifetime twice that long.

Sherwood served as the pastor of Bayside of South Sacramento and had an outsize impact on the community, one that echoed his physical size. Sherwood was larger than life in every way and impacted our region far beyond the congregation he so faithfully served. Two days after his tragic death, our region's largest newspaper, the *Sacramento Bee*, published an editorial that spoke volumes about Sherwood's hard-won influence. The editorial carried the headline "Building on Bishop Carthen's Legacy Is the Challenge We Now Face."

And what a legacy it is: Chaplain of the NBA's Sacramento Kings, where he was lovingly known as "The Rev." Architect of the city's Cops and Clergy program, which created partnerships between members of law enforcement and clergy to stem gang violence (Sherwood called it "Hug-a-Thug"). A leading voice in United Pastors of Sacramento, a coalition of African American churches. Founder and director of Our Family Community Foundation, a nonprofit organization designed to help parents and children obtain educational, tutorial, and social opportunities. A longtime force in the community to assist the homeless—the day before he died, Sherwood spoke at a fundraiser aimed at ending homelessness. The list goes on. And on. And on.

When Sacramento Police chief Sam Somers learned the news, he and several of his senior officers rushed to the hospital.

"I was crushed," the chief told the *Bee*. "I admired him greatly, a man full of love, full of compassion. He was here to make a difference."

Yes, Sherwood Carthen was here to make a difference—and he set out to make that difference far beyond the walls of his beloved church. Our community noticed. How many influential newspapers would say about the death of a local pastor, as *The Bee* did about Sherwood, "His passing leaves a spiritual void in our community and a huge civic gap that will be very hard to bridge"?

Sherwood cared deeply about God, and because of this, he also cared about the people in his community. That is why he dedicated his too-short life to serving both. He left behind "a grateful city that is kinder, healthier and safer because of his good works," declared the *Bee*. And then the newspaper concluded, "The community's challenge now is to build on Carthen's legacy with the same spirit and determination that he embodied."[1]

The challenge really belongs to us all. If your heart beats in sync with the heart of Jesus, then you must come to see that He calls you and me and every Christian to bring *hope* to our communities, wherever they are.

I Had No Clue

A few years ago, I was talking to Sherwood when he shook his head and said, "Ray, I don't think you get that the schools in my part of town are different from the schools in your suburban part of town."

That can't be true, I thought.

I took the bait. Sherwood's challenge bothered me so much that, without telling anybody, I took a whole day off to drive around Sacramento, cruising by every elementary school I could find. What I saw shocked me. Sherwood was right. I had no clue.

I saw schools with rows of shattered windows, schools with no playgrounds, schools with dangerous parking lots that screamed, "Stay out!" I even saw a couple of schools with no air-conditioning—*in blistering Sacramento!* The more I saw, the angrier I got.

If Christians and others in this community don't rise up and go after this, I thought, *it's not going to get fixed.*

I'd already been to the Bible study where I received the challenge from Acts 2 that the church has to bring good deeds to a community in order for the community to receive the good news. I had the motivation to start Serve Weekend, which I mentioned in the previous chapter. Now I had the target.

"Okay, we have to do something," I said, in an urgent meeting I called with Sherwood. We started kicking around some ideas, and the whole plan unfolded. I said, "What about this? What if we shut down our churches occasionally, rent out ARCO Arena, and have one massive worship service instead? Then we could raise some money for the schools and help as many of them as possible."

We went for it. We interviewed all the principals in the area, identified the neediest schools, packed ARCO Arena, and raised almost four hundred thousand dollars. To date, we have helped rebuild six Sacramento schools.

Especially today, I recognize that none of this would have happened unless Sherwood Carthen had challenged me, saying in essence, "Ray, you need to get a clue."

We have a lot of work left to do, but it's a start. Now, we have workers branching out into all kinds of community services. Here are just a couple of their stories.

Rescuing the Future—One Kid at a Time

During the process of working with these schools, we made a startling discovery. Turns out that the state of California determines the number of prison beds it will need in the future by looking at current third-grade reading levels. In other words, the single best predictor for estimating the state's future number of criminals is the number of third-grade kids who currently read below their grade level. Unbelievable!

The corollary news was that if a struggling third grader gets a reading tutor, he or she can not only catch up but bypass the target reading level *within just eighteen months*—an improvement that completely changes their future direction.

Bring on Mary. Mary wanted to be useful, so she prayed a little prayer: *God, this year let me profoundly affect just one person's life for the better.* Months later, at a regular worship service, we described these dramatic ill effects of illiteracy. We called for volunteers and she thought, *My kids are too old to read to, but I always loved it.* Then she heard that volunteers didn't need any special qualifications, so she thought, *I would love to make a difference in the life of a child.*

Mary had no background in teaching and felt completely unqualified for the job, but a small amount of training gave her a step-by-step plan of how to proceed. Mary headed from her suburban home into downtown Sacramento for her first day of tutoring. Mary was paired with a fourth grader named Betsy and started working with her twice a week, for forty-five minutes each session. During her thirty-minute drive to Betsy's school, Mary ordinarily would have had music playing. But the responsibility of tutoring a little girl felt so weighty, she prayed each day, asking God the same request—to let her make a difference.

"I immediately felt a connection with Betsy," Mary said. "I was thrilled to be partnered with her. After about the third week, I could tell that she was connecting with me too. We formed this really, really great friendship. She tried her hardest because she wanted to please me, and I tried my hardest because I wanted to help her."

Betsy started fourth grade at two or three grade levels below the state's benchmarks. By the end of that school year, after just nine months with Mary, she scored *above* her grade level.

"I was blown away," Mary said. "God *used* me—someone with no qualifications whatsoever—to help this child. He answered my prayer! When I started, I felt like I had my hand up waving and calling out, 'Pick me! Please pick me! Use me to make a difference in someone else's life!' And then He truly, truly answered that prayer. It was a super cool experience."

The "Tour de Sacramento"

A couple in our church, Shawn and Kelly, came from diverse backgrounds. Kelly received Christ and renounced the Mormon Church she'd been raised in, then insisted Shawn attend her new church, Bayside. At first, it was mildly entertaining. Shawn was an atheist but also an athlete, and some of our church's sports activities intrigued him. Before long, he made the decision to follow Christ too. Then he sat back for a couple of years to figure out what it was all about. Shawn wrote:

> In 2008, Kelly and I heard a message by Francis Chan on "lukewarm Christianity" that spoke to our core. We fit the definition to a tee. So, we made a life-changing decision to downsize our life (house, cars, stuff . . .) and more fully devote our lives to Christ. Kelly focused on growing her ministry to people leaving the Mormon Church, and I focused on what to focus on. I didn't have even one idea.
>
> Two months later, I received an invitation from the Bayside Homeless Ministry looking for volunteers to make sandwiches and sort clothing. I didn't think anything of it until Saturday morning when I woke up earlier than normal with a strong feeling that I should go. Kelly thought I was crazy. During the outreach, after all of the food and clothing were gone, I noticed many of the homeless pushing and riding bicycles.
>
> I love bikes and grew up riding, racing, and working on bikes when I wasn't working in my dad's auto repair shop. Ironically, his shop was located next to a mission, complete with the "Jesus Saves" sign out front. I used to harass the homeless people who frequented the area. But on this Saturday, I talked with one of the homeless people pushing a broken bike. I learned the importance of the bike for her life. Bicycles enable homeless

people to get to shelters, get food, find and keep jobs, get medical care, and just get around.

I fixed her bike right then with some tools I kept in the back of my car. And right there, Cycles 4 Hope was born. I finally realized my purpose and talents and discovered the plans Christ had for me, to serve people in need. Friends helped me write a mission statement: "Providing hope, independence, and opportunity with something as simple as a bicycle and a message of hope."

I didn't quit my day job to launch the ministry. By simplifying our lives and using the time it frees up for God's work, in these few years, we have been able to give away or repair thousands and thousands of bicycles. I prefer to count our success by the number of smiles we create when someone rides by on a new or repaired Cycles 4 Hope bike. The most important thing we've done is to restore hope and joy in the lives of people. Hope because they know someone cares about, loves, and sees value in them. Joy because a bicycle provides freedom to get away from the troubles of their lives and enjoy the world God created and the life He gave them.

One Thousand and Counting

Dan Lott worked in the computer technology business. Over the years, he went through four job transitions and had a total of fifteen months without work. He retired in 1999 and unofficially began mentoring professionals who were going through job transitions.

After nine years of retirement, he made a goal to volunteer more than he golfed. At a church meeting one day, someone asked how the church could better support professionals, specifically people going through job transitions. The next thing Dan knew, he was having coffee with Hal Reisiger, head of a career jobs ministry at Saddleback Church in Lake Forest, California. Dan realized that if anything were going to happen at Bayside, he would have to lead it. Hal loaded him up with documents he'd need, and Dan headed home.

Dan launched the program in 2009 with twenty-five volunteers from the church. The first night it opened, 165 people showed up seeking assistance. Today, Bayside Career Coaching holds weekly seminars for teaching, encouragement, and practice; offers one-on-one coaching sessions; and hosts networking nights to connect employers and workers. To date, the program has helped more than one thousand job seekers find paid work.

"By bringing somebody into the program, instead of them traveling alone, we give them hope," Dan said. "There's a team of people to help them and cheer them on. We lift them up and give them the confidence to effectively communicate about themselves to potential employers. It's the best job I've ever had."

Part of what keeps Dan going are the upbeat notes of gratitude from happy, successful job seekers, like this:

> My job search has been agonizing . . . many nights of sleep lost . . . depression . . . loss of appetite . . . most discouraging. I applied to at least 3 jobs daily. When I wouldn't get a reply, I would pray. Bayside Career Coaching helped me to focus my strengths on what I do best . . . what I love . . . what I know I am good at. I wanted to find a job that I could grow with and stay with for many years to come.
>
> I just never dreamed God would give the perfect job. I am happy to tell you that [a store] has hired me to *manage* their counter. I have held 5 other positions in cosmetics, and loved what I did. To be doing what I love, I owe it all to God. He has changed my heart and the way I view people and hardships. THANK YOU!

Until We Meet Again

As I think of the countless opportunities we have to reach out in service to our community, my mind inevitably drifts back to my friend Sherwood Carthen. To me, he epitomized a man who loves Jesus and who therefore loves the people in his community. Jesus told us that the Great Commandment really has two parts: to love God with all our hearts, souls, minds, and spirits, *and* to love our neighbors as ourselves.

Sherwood lived that.

On the day of Sherwood's death, Sacramento mayor Kevin Johnson issued an official statement that said, "Today we lost a special friend, a loving father, a committed husband and a great leader who led not only with powerful words from the pulpit, but by extending his ministry beyond the walls of the church."[2]

For decades, Sherwood Carthen led in countless ways. He led marches against drive-by shootings, and he hosted public forums on crime and social issues. Why? Because he loved his community. And he loved Jesus. And he felt convinced that the two things belonged together.

That's why DeAngelo Mack of the Sacramento Violence Intervention Program could say of my friend, "He had the respect of all his colleagues in the clergy and the respect of young men and women on the street. He was all about the community."[3]

I loved Sherwood Carthen. I will miss him terribly. But the work goes on. The divine call remains unchanged. God created us to love Him and to love our neighbors. I know that one day I will see Sherwood again. And when I do, I want to be able to tell him, "Buddy, I finally got a clue. And I have you to thank for that."

Until we meet again, my friend.

17.

UNLEASHING HOPE IN THE WORLD

Let the little children come to me, and do not hinder them, for the kingdom of heaven belongs to such as these.

MATTHEW 19:14

Every child you encounter is a divine appointment.

WESS STAFFORD,

FORMER PRESIDENT AND CEO

OF COMPASSION INTERNATIONAL

Not long ago, I was on a plane and picked up a copy of the airline's *Sky Mall* magazine. This catalog sells some cool, edgy stuff and some stuff that goes right over the edge. As I flipped through the magazine, I saw this cat sitting on a toilet seat staring at me. (I am not making this up!) I stopped and read the ad. For fifty dollars, you could buy an attachment for your toilet seat to teach your cat to use the toilet. Yeah. You're thinking what I thought.

Believe me, I know *lots* of cat lovers. But not one of the cat owners I know has ever bought equipment to train his or her cat to use the toilet at home. Even if they did, I wonder, is this really the best thing a cat lover can do with fifty dollars?

It reminds me of the guy who spent twenty million dollars on a home in Lake Tahoe that had eleven bathrooms. I guess when you've got to go, you got to go *fast*. Then there's the professional basketball player who installed an automated teller machine in his kitchen because he didn't like having to look for one. Or the lady who purchased a diamond-encrusted Bluetooth headset for fifty thousand dollars. Or the executive who got a leather, gold, and silver Monopoly game for Christmas that cost seven thousand dollars.

It's been said that Americans buy things we don't need with money we don't have to impress people we don't like.

Now, this chapter might cost you something. But it might also be the greatest ride of your life. You can learn how to take the money you've been spending on some small, silly purchase every month and turn it into unleashing hope that has the power to change the world.

I believe that the smartest thing you can do with your life is to make things happen that wouldn't have existed without you.

I've given you a lot of illustrations about people who did exactly that. There were the girls who gave their shoes to the woman in Mexico. There were the people who got together to liberate the young women caught in the sex trade industry in Cambodia. There were the high school students who filled Pringles cans with cash and raised fifty thousand dollars to launch a child survival program in another country.

For every story I told, there are a thousand I didn't tell you. You know what's even better than reading a cool story? *Being* the story. This can happen through anyone—including you! Let me give you six reasons.

Changing the World Has Never Been More Possible

We live in a time when the potential for changing the world has never been higher. With today's technology, things can happen very rapidly.

About a year ago, I was invited to speak at the international gathering of the staff of Compassion International. The highlight for me was listening to a message from a brilliant leader, Dr. Scott Todd. He started by telling an old story about starfish, but he added a startling twist. You've probably heard the story. It was written in 1969 by Loren Eiseley, called "The Star Thrower." The short version goes like this:

An old man had a habit of early morning walks on the beach. One day, after a storm, he saw a girl reaching down to the sand, picking up starfish and very gently throwing them into the ocean.

"Young lady," he asked, "Why are you throwing starfish into the ocean?"

"The sun is up, and the tide is going out, and if I don't throw them in, they will die."

"But there are miles and miles of beach and starfish all along it. You cannot possibly make a difference."

The young woman listened politely, then bent down, picked up another starfish and threw it into the sea. She said, "It made a difference to that one."[1]

Scott then told a new version of that story:

A man was walking along the beach when he saw a girl taking a picture of a starfish with her iPhone. Approaching the girl, he asked, "What are you doing?"

"Uploading pictures of these stranded starfish to my Facebook page and asking friends to tweet the call to action," she said. "The surf is up and the tide is going out. If I can get enough friends out here, we can get all these starfish back into the water before sunset."

"Little girl," the man asked, "what does tweet mean?"

The girl rolled her eyes. She bent down, picked up a starfish, and threw it back into the surf. Then she gave the man a wry, twinkly-eyed smile and said, "If you want to help out, this is how you do it."

Within hours, thousands of children stormed the beach and every starfish was rescued!

Scott's point: *things are possible now that have never been possible before in human history!* You and I live in a day and age when, because of connectivity, change can occur at a rate that for most of human history was unthinkable. Nations have been overthrown in six months. Diseases are being eradicated. Historic changes are happening rapidly that were never before possible. We live in exciting times.

One Person Can Unleash Hope in the World

The world has always been changed by individuals. History books are filled with stories about the lives of one person after another who did something that impacted the world. Abraham Lincoln unleashed hope in the world when he stepped up to the presidency, knowing it could cost his life, and won freedom for millions. Clara Barton was so shy, her parents sent her to a special school. But she became the first woman leader hired by the federal government, helped Civil War soldiers, and started the Red Cross, unleashing a legacy of hope for millions worldwide. German businessman Oskar Schindler caroused with Nazi soldiers while hiding and saving Jews right under their noses. He unleashed hope in countless lives around the world.

A high schooler named Toby wrote an essay on world hunger and won a spot on a two-and-a-half-week study tour through Africa. Toby marveled at Ethiopia's beauty, but also at its rampant poverty. One day he visited a distribution camp to hand out food and supplies and play with some local kids. As the bus driver beckoned Toby to leave, an eleven-year-old boy tapped him on the shoulder. The boy stared at Toby's T-shirt, and then looked down at his own shirt—thin, dirty, and filled with holes. His look said it all: *Can I have your shirt?*

Toby had not come prepared. His luggage was a long way off. Giving the boy his shirt would mean Toby would be exposed to the blistering African sun for the rest of the day. The bus driver honked. Toby backed away from the boy, shrugged his shoulders, and stepped onto the bus.

As the bus drove away, the weight of that single request gripped Toby. That night, he couldn't stop thinking about an eleven-year-old boy who just wanted a T-shirt like those that filled Toby's closet and drawers back home. As he thought, Toby kept hearing one sentence Jesus had said: "Whatever you did for one of the least of these brothers and sisters of mine, you did for me" (Matthew 25:40).

Toby waited until everyone went to sleep, then he broke down and sobbed. The memory of that scene haunted Toby when he returned to Michigan. Toby thought about people in America who used T-shirts to wash cars and clean windows. He resolved to do something. He organized a T-shirt drive called "Give The Shirt Off Your Back."

Toby collected T-shirts door-to-door. He persuaded stores to set bins outside for collecting T-shirts. Local media gave the story some airtime. The next thing Toby knew, it seemed like everybody in the state of Michigan was giving him T-shirts. He collected ten thousand of them.

Then he had another problem. How do you get two tons of T-shirts from Michigan to Ethiopia? He called one relief agency after another but received the same answer: "We'd love to help, but shipping is too expensive." How expensive? He called United Parcel Service and learned for himself: sixty-five thousand dollars.

Finally, someone put Toby in touch with an outfit called Supporters of Sub-Sahara Africa. They happened to be taking a shipment of supplies to Africa and they agreed to take Toby's T-shirts. There was just one catch. They were going only to one country. They asked him, "Is it okay if these shirts go to Ethiopia?"

Toby doesn't know exactly where those T-shirts ended up, but he hopes one of them ended up in the hands of a certain boy.

"I'll never forget that kid," he said. "I know it's unlikely he'll get one of the shirts I sent. What are the odds of that? But I can pray. God can do *anything*."[2]

This teenager chose making history over making money and is now unleashing hope in thousands of lives.

The World Can Change—One Child at a Time

I believe that whoever changes today's kids changes tomorrow's future. Some years ago I was on another plane (they all look alike inside). I chatted with the man sitting next to me and learned that he audited relief agencies. There are some great groups doing great works. I know the leaders of a lot of them, and I admire them deeply. So of course I wanted to know which ones were the best or the worst! And of course he wouldn't say. But as we were walking off the flight, he introduced me to Compassion International. I looked them up and was intrigued with the organization. Their mission statement is, "Releasing children from poverty in Jesus' name." I like that, because I believe that the best way to win the future is to focus on reaching young people.

Whoever wins the kids wins the culture. Whoever wins the kids wins the nation. Whoever wins the kids ultimately *wins*. I believe our best focus is on children. I believe it is possible to rescue thousands of children out of poverty. I believe it is possible to rescue millions of them. For that reason, and many others, our church became involved.

I told a few people about Compassion, then a few more. At this time, Bayside Church people sponsor eight thousand children through Compassion International. That number will have grown by the time you read this, and I hope it will grow exponentially as a few more people read this. The reason people at our church sponsor those kids is that without sponsors, eight thousand kids would still face a future where they've not broken the cycle of poverty.

The Compassion sponsoring model is the most cost-effective way I've found to change a community and break a pattern. It's one to one. One person *here* unleashes hope in one life *there*. Right now it costs thirty-eight dollars a month. Last time I checked, that's two movie tickets and a bucket of popcorn. It's two large pizzas. By the time you read this, that's probably equal to one gallon of gas (at least here in California!).

With that one sponsorship of thirty-eight dollars, the child receives food, clothes, immunizations, ongoing medical care, and even school. Where there are no schools, the children get job training. In the places I've traveled in the world, if children are born in poverty they cannot get out of poverty because they can't get an education. School costs money. So if you don't have money, you can't go to school, so you can't break the cycle.

The best way to create a generation of future leaders is to grab a bunch of kids who don't take opportunities for granted, educate them, and then turn them loose. The way Compassion does this, if someone sponsors a child, that child gets to go to school. If the child tests well, he or she gets a sponsor to go on to high school. If the child tests well there, Compassion finds sponsors to pay for those children to go to the university. But it all begins with one person giving thirty-eight dollars per month. What can happen with one child is astonishing.

Let me tell you about my friend Solomon. Solomon grew up in the Massai tribe in Kenya. His dad lives with several wives, each of whom has a hut. There is no school in the area. No running water. No electricity. This tribe has lived for thousands of years in grinding poverty. I visit here every year. It's like taking a trip back to the Stone Age.

But someone came here seventeen years ago and decided to help a boy who could never repay them. For thirty-eight dollars a month, this young man grew up with good nutrition, good values, and good study habits, and eventually graduated from the University of Nairobi. With a degree in his hand, he had the world before him. He could have written his ticket to do anything from that point. Instead, he went back to his own village. Solomon started a Compassion International program in that village. He now has 330 children in his Massai village on the very same path he was on.

"Solomon," I said one day. "Why are you doing this?"

"Because I want every child from my tribe to have the same opportunity to escape poverty that I was given."

Solomon didn't stop there. He started raising money to build their first-ever elementary school. The building he was going to use burned down. So he called his buddy Ray in the States and said, "Can you help us?"

I took it to the church and a whole crowd of our people paid their way over there and built the first elementary school building in the history of that area. Hundreds of kids every day are getting an education in that elementary school. It all started with one person helping one boy—Solomon.

One person can unleash hope in the world, one child at a time.

Something Is Better than Nothing

My friend Mike Yaconelli was a lifelong friend and one of the most encouraging guys on the planet. One of the things I heard him say over and over was this: Quit feeling guilty about not doing everything. But do something . . . *because something is better than nothing!*

A pastor in Korea with Lou Gehrig's disease named Jungha Kim went to a conference where hundreds of balloons were dropped from the ceiling. He thought inside the balloons there were gifts of some kind, so he grabbed five. Instead, the announcer said that each balloon had a child's name that needed to be supported by a sponsorship. Pastor Kim did not have money and was sponsoring two children already, but he didn't want to give up those balloons either, so he prayed for a way to sponsor seven children. He remembered that as a boy he had shined shoes, so he set up a shoe-shine stand in front of his church to make the extra money he needed to care for those kids.

As Pastor Kim shined shoes, he prayed specifically for the future of each child. He prayed for Zenabou in Burkina Faso to be a lawmaker. For Luis in Ecuador to become a doctor. For Eric in Kenya to become a great politician. For Jesus in Peru to become a pastor. For Ikenshia in El Salvador to become a leader in her country. For Zharick in Colombia to become Miss Colombia. For Joel in Bolivia to become a general in the army.

The disease has now kept Pastor Kim from being able to shine enough shoes to sponsor the children. But other people have stepped in and helped him keep the sponsorships going. Even in his debilitated condition, his face shines when he talks about his seven children and their futures.[3]

Unleashing Hope Brings a Huge Reward

Francis Chan electrified the crowd at a Thrive conference a few years ago with this story. He started by reading aloud a passage of Scripture: "When the Son of Man comes in his glory, and all the angels with him, he will sit on his glorious throne. All the nations will be gathered before him, and he will separate the people one from another as a shepherd separates the sheep from the goats. He will put the sheep on his right and the goats on his left" (Matthew 25:31–33).

Francis said he was at a camp recently and someone pointed out a sixteen-year-old girl who supported several needy kids in other countries. He went over to meet her.

"Hey, your counselor told me you support kids. How many do you sponsor?"

"Fourteen," she said.

"You're still in high school! How in the world do you sponsor fourteen kids?"

"I work," she said. "I have three jobs in the summers. Waiting tables, baby-sitting, and being a lifeguard."

"And *all* your money goes to the fourteen kids?"

"Yeah."

Then Francis said something I'll never forget. He said, "I'm so grateful for that sixteen-year-old girl who is supporting fourteen kids. She thinks saving fourteen lives is better than saving money for a car. People might think she's crazy, but I think she's right because at any moment now the Son of God is coming down from the sky in all His glory. Not in a human or a veiled form, but in *all* His glory with a hundred million angels. Can you imagine? He grabs all the people and starts to separate them. Now, is that girl stupid? At that point, is she crazy?"

> Then the King will say to those on his right, "Come, you who are blessed by my Father; take your inheritance, the kingdom prepared for you since the creation of the world. For I was hungry and you gave me something to eat, I was thirsty and you gave me something to drink, I was a stranger and you invited me in, I needed clothes and you clothed me, I was sick and you looked after me, I was in prison and you came to visit me."
>
> Then the righteous will answer him, "Lord, when did we see you hungry and feed you, or thirsty and give you something to drink? When did we see you a stranger and invite you in, or needing clothes and clothe you? When did we see you sick or in prison and go to visit you?"
>
> The King will reply, "Truly I tell you, whatever you did for one of the least of these brothers and sisters of mine, you did for me." (Matthew 25:34–40)

A Lot of People Can Unleash Hope in a Lot of Lives

So far, Bayside has sponsored children from twenty-five countries: Bangladesh, Bolivia, Brazil, Burkina Faso, Colombia, Dominican Republic, East India,

Ecuador, El Salvador, Ethiopia, Ghana, Guatemala, Haiti, Honduras, India, Indonesia, Kenya, Mexico, Nicaragua, Peru, Philippines, Rwanda, Tanzania, Thailand, and Uganda. What do all these countries have in common? They all have a better future than they would have if these children were not being helped.

I told you it might cost some money to read this chapter, because I'm inviting you to join me. We've put together a website, HopeQuotient.com— maybe you've been on it already to take the hope assessment. On there, we're doing something that's pretty cool. We're going to double the number of children Bayside has sponsored by opening the opportunity to everyone reading this book. I invite you to join "Ray's Team" and sponsor a child through Compassion International. It's not hard.

An eleven-year-old named Ben in Australia heard about the Compassion kids and decided he wanted to sponsor a child. So he thought about what he could do. He created a flyer and invited people who wanted their dogs walked to allow him to walk their dogs. He walked two dogs on a school night, and five dogs on Saturdays. Then the business built up. People without dogs started thinking of odd jobs he could do for them, like sweeping.

Ben is twelve now. He said, "I like to give good customer service. I get there five minutes early and leave five minutes late. When I walk their dogs, I always tell them their dog has been well behaved."

He has now fully paid for two children for a year. Ben set new goals. Now he's trying to raise six thousand dollars to build a well in one of the villages where one of his kids lives.[4]

Maybe you can't find time to add one more job to your list. But you can empty a storage unit and free up eighty dollars per month. That's more than enough for two kids. Or work it out a month at a time. One month say no to the manicurist who offers you the forty-dollar-plus paraffin treatment. Choose Netflix over forty dollars for two movie tickets and a bucket of popcorn. Or eat leftovers instead of buying two pizzas for forty dollars.

Becoming the story in history is more available than you think. Unleashing hope in the world is easier than you think when you unleash hope one child at a time.

One of my hopes for this book is that it would result in a wave of tens of thousands of children around the world being lifted out of poverty and given a brand-new, bright future because people who read *Hope Quotient* practiced unleashing hope!

Join us and sponsor a child—sponsor several if you want—and break the grip of poverty for a family in one generation. Just go to www.HopeQuotient.com and I'll show you how! The world is waiting for you to unleash your hope. I hope you will.

READ THIS LAST:
A CONSPIRACY OF GRACE

I heard a Chicago area pastor describe what he says was "the most emotional day of his life." It occurred on his very first day of playing Little League baseball. All sixty of his Iowa relatives showed up to watch him play. This is how he told it . . .

The pressure was off the charts—and it kept getting worse. My first ever Little League baseball game. I'm the youngest guy on the team. I'm the least skilled on the team. And I'm the skinniest guy on the team. My uniform hung off my scrawny body like a rag.

I played right field. Even when you're only eight years old, you know why you're in right field. You're there because never in the recorded history of Little League has a ball been hit to right field.

I came up to bat three times and struck out every time. I never even touched the ball.

It was the seventh and last inning, the bases were loaded, and our team was behind by one run. I was up. I stood in the on-deck circle and heard someone say, "Hey, Coach, pinch hit!" The coach came up to me and said, "Get up there and take your swing." I walked what seemed like fifty miles to home plate. I got up there, scared stiff. I was shaking, and the second I looked out at the pitcher's mound, I knew I had no shot. The pitcher stood at least six feet, nine inches tall and sported a full beard—at least, that's how a ten-year-old looked to an eight-year-old. I stepped into the batter's box still shaking.

Everybody in the place was standing up and screaming.

The noise was deafening.

The pitcher wound up. I didn't even see his first pitch. *Whoosh!* I heard it come, heard it hit the catcher's mitt, heard the umpire yell, "Strike one!"

The catcher tossed the ball back out to the pitcher's mound. The pitcher wound up and threw his second pitch—*Whoosh!* I heard the ball hit the mitt. "Strike two!"

As the ball went back to the mound one more time, I said to myself, "I gotta do something or this game's over!"

So I stepped out of the batter's box, took my bat, and hit my shoes with it. I didn't know why, but I'd seen others do it. And then I made a mistake—I looked around. Here's what I saw: Two hundred people on their side, standing up and screaming for me to strike out and lose the game. And on the other side I saw two hundred people, including sixty of my relatives, standing up and screaming for me to get a hit and win the game. Some people were actually hanging on the fence and straddling the fence and screaming for me to get a hit and win the game. I had never felt pressure like that. I thought, *If I don't get a hit, I will be a failure and everybody that I know will know I'm a failure.*

Shaking, I stepped back into the box, and said to myself, "I gotta get a hit—I'm gonna get a hit." So for the first time ever, I swung. I actually started swinging during the pitcher's windup. The pitch came in, I saw it, and I swung as hard as I could.

I . . .

Missed . . .

I heard the ball hit the catcher's mitt, and I heard the umpire say, "Strike three, you're out! Game over." A huge cheer erupted from two hundred people.

Then I heard something else that I will never forget—an audible groan from two hundred other people—and I knew I had failed. I had let everybody down. I was going to have to live with this failure for the rest of my life.

I dropped the bat at home plate and started the longest walk of my life, up the first-base line to the dugout. The other team gathered and started chanting, "Two, four, six, eight, who do we appreciate? *Him!*" I walked by my opponents, down to the dugout, and heard my own teammates say, "Loser!" "Idiot!" "You lost the game, moron!" (You know how sensitive ten-year-old boys are!) I walked past them to the end of the dugout. I sat down, pulled my hat over my eyes, threw my jacket over my head, and sobbed for probably fifteen minutes. Nobody came anywhere near me.

It was the last game of the day, the dust was settling, and I could hear the gravel underneath car tires as people pulled out of the parking lot. Then everything got quiet. I continued to sit there, crying. I knew I would never, *ever* recover from this failure.

Then, I heard a noise from the pitcher's mound. A voice said, "Hey, son, get back up. The game ain't over."

I didn't move.

Then I heard it again, louder: "Son, get back up. The game ain't over."

I heard it a third time, louder still: "Son, get back up. The game ain't over!"

I pulled off my coat and pulled up my cap and looked out. It took a minute for my tear-filled eyes to readjust to the light. Sure enough, there on the pitcher's mound stood my dad. He was wearing a mitt and holding a ball, and he said again, "Son, get back up. The game ain't over."

I looked and saw that none of my relatives had left. They were all in the field, waiting to play. A bunch of toddlers with their diapers hanging loose were waddling around the infield. Aunt Emma stood out in left field. My blind uncle Joe, trying to find right field, ran into the fence. They were all out there, and my dad stood on the pitcher's mound, calmly saying, "Hey, son. Get back up. The game ain't over. Get back up."

I looked toward home plate. My bat was still lying where I had dropped it. I sheepishly walked over to the plate. My dad was so cool. He just said, "Son, the game ain't over."

He threw a pitch, everybody started cheering . . . and I missed.

He threw it again. I missed again.

About fifteen pitches later, my dad threw it right down the middle and I went *whack!* and knocked it into left field. I stood at home plate, and my dad said, "What are you doing? Run!"

Okay, where's first base? I'd never been there. I ran down to first base, just in time to see Aunt Emma, the left fielder, throw the ball into center field. I thought, *Cool, I'm going to get a double!* I ran to second base, just in time to see Todd, a pretty good athlete playing center field, throw the ball into right field. As I ran to third base, I think I suspected they were screwing up on purpose. It was what I call now *a conspiracy of grace* to make sure I got home safe. But at this point, all I knew was, they've thrown the ball to a blind guy *and I'm gonna score!*

I rounded third and sprinted toward home. When I got about ten feet away, I dove for the plate, slid across, and jumped up. I dusted myself off, feeling good for the first time in four hours.

And then I saw him. About five feet in front of me was my dad. He'd gotten down on one knee, so we were the same height. Tears were streaming down his face. My dad held out his arms and said, "Son, you're safe at home." I threw myself into his arms. He picked me up and whispered in my ear, "I told you the game wasn't over."

That day turned into one of the best days of my life. My relatives ran onto the infield and, as the sun set on this little baseball field in Nowhere, Iowa, they carried me off the field, cheering.

The central invitation of the Bible is to develop a hope-giving relationship with God, who, if He could get your attention for a few minutes, would say to you these words: "Get back up. The game's not over." I believe God means it when he says, "I am the Lord; those who hope in me will not be disappointed" (Isaiah 49:23).

Several years ago, I received a surprising call from *Forbes* magazine. An editor said, "We would like to do an interview with you."

"You're the magazine for millionaires," I said. "You must have the wrong guy!"

"We would like to do an interview about what CEOs of corporations could learn from the pastors of thriving churches," he said.

"Why me?"

"Because the church you lead has sustained a consistent growth rate for fifteen straight years. Most CEOs would like to have that happen in their companies, so we want to know what kind of factors make that happen."

"Are you kidding me? *Yes!*"

Two hours later, the final question they asked was a great question. "What's the most important thing you have learned in the last ten years?"

"That's easy," I said. "I've learned a lot, but the most important life leadership lesson I've learned in the past decade is that the solution to everything is the right person. In a company, on a team, for a church, when the right person arrives and is in charge, everything goes well. And when the wrong person arrives, things do not go well.

"Anything that is not in good shape is one really great person away from being in good shape. And the opposite is true. Anything that is in good shape is one wrong person away from falling into decline. In the Bible, when the nation has the right king, the people thrive. When they have the wrong leader, it declines.

"The solution to everything is to have the right person."

I was able to be emphatic with the interviewer because that one principle is the central message of the entire Bible. The solution to everything is not the right religion. It's not the right ritual. It *is* the right person. That person, for your life, is Jesus Christ.

If you read this book and realized that you don't have the right resources to make hope rise in your life, then I have a final message for you. God wants you to have every spiritual resource you could ever need, and that's why He sent His Son, Jesus Christ.

Perhaps you're thinking right now, *I would love to live on the power of God. I would love to have my past forgiven and be able to let go. I would love to have the rest of my life be the best of my life. I would love to live in the presence of God and have the power of God. I would love to have a friendship with God.*

This is the very reason that Jesus Christ came to this earth. The solution to those needs is not religion or ritual, but a relationship with Jesus Christ. Jesus came to earth because He wanted to have a relationship with *you*. How do you do that? It's simpler than you think. He's just waiting for you to invite Him into your life. The following prayer will help you start. Pray it right out loud.

Dear God, thank You for sending Your Son, Jesus Christ, into the world. I believe Jesus is who He said He was and proved it by rising from death. I want to get to know You personally. Thank You for Jesus dying for me and forgiving all my sins. Please forgive me for all of those sins and come into my life. I receive You as my Lord and Savior. Thank You for Your free gift of eternal life. Amen.

If you prayed that prayer, I want to welcome you to the greatest adventure of your life. To help you get started with a solid foundation, e-mail me at PastorRay@HopeQuotient.com, and I'll give you *free* resources to get you started. Why would I do that? Because I believe that a relationship with God will start everything new for you. And because I have high hopes for you.

ACKNOWLEDGMENTS

Every person I know is looking for what this book provides—*hope*!
The following people have given me exactly that in the seven-year development of this project. Here they are . . .

To Steve Halliday: The first draft of this book took weeks of conversation and writing. You are a brilliant, talented writer and thinker. This book is better because of your insights and writing. Thank you!

To my cowriter, Joann Webster: Your energy, positive spirit, and grace were just what we needed. You consistently went the extra mile for this project while being a joy to work with. Thank you!

To project coordinator, Rick Nash: You are just what I expected from a Harvard/Dallas Theological Seminary grad. Great theology and brilliance. Without you this project would not have gotten off the ground.

To Dr. William Brown, Regent University: Your terrific work on the HQ assessment is just what people need to build hope.

To Rick Christian and Joel Kneedler at Alive Communications: I love the way Alive Communications honors God and inspires people. I can't imagine two better guys to be partnered with.

To Debbie Wickwire and the folks at Thomas Nelson: For being people of vision, class, excellence, and *fun*, I am grateful. This is proving to be a great partnership. Thank you.

To John Volinsky, John Harris, Scott Shaull, David Durham, and Lincoln

Brewster: Nothing is impossible when the five of you are in the room. Thanks for your friendship and partnership. I love doing life and ministry with you!

To Dena Davidson, Justin Boatman, Candy Brown, Dave Eaton, and Jordan Honnette: Your critical help at critical moments made all the difference.

To Darlene Anderson: You remember everything, serve everyone, and are a joy to work with. Without you . . . well, I don't even want to think about it!

To my executive assistant Donna Bostwick: Carol and I are honored to have you in our lives. If you don't do what you do—there is no way we could do what God has called us to. Thank you for keeping the universe and me running.

And to my four kids—Mark, Scott, Christy, and Leslie: You were a blast to raise and are even more fun as adults. No dad ever had it better and I am prouder of you than you will ever know! Keep turning out like Mom!

NOTES

Read This Second

1. Daniel Goleman, *Emotional Intelligence* (New York: Bantam Books, 1995).

Chapter 1: Where It Began

1. L. C. Naden, *Christ Is the Answer* (Warburton, Victoria, Australia: Signs Publishing Company, 1950), 5.

Chapter 2: Your HQ Changes Everything

1. Laura Hillenbrand, *Unbroken* (New York: Random House, 2010).
2. Ibid., 321.
3. Louis Zamperini, personal conversation with the author, February 17, 2011.
4. Hillenbrand, *Unbroken,* 376.
5. Ibid., 399.
6. Ibid., 384.
7. Louis Zamperini, personal conversation with the author, February 17, 2011.
8. D. James Kennedy and Jerry Newcombe, *What If Jesus Had Never Been Born?* (Nashville: Thomas Nelson, 1994), 3–4.
9. 2 Kings 4:28; Lamentations 3:21; Romans 15:13; 2 Thessalonians 2:16; Ruth 1:12; Job 14:19.
10. Job 11:18; Psalm 9:18; Isaiah 57:10.

Chapter 3: Discouragement Destroys Everything

1. Rick Warren, *God's Answers to Life's Difficult Questions* (Grand Rapids: Zondervan, 2006), 93.

2. For background on this urban legend, see Barbara Mikkelson, "Cow Tao," Snopes.com, February 14, 2011, http://www.snopes.com/critters/farce /cowtao.asp. Pastor Ray has dramatized details in his retelling.

3. Rene Pol Nevils and Deborah George Hardy, *Ignatius Rising: The Life of John Kennedy Toole* (New Orleans: Louisiana State University Press, 2001).

Chapter 4: The Seven

1. Staff of the NY Times, *The Night the Lights Went Out* (New York: Signet Books, 1965).

2. Norman Vincent Peale, *The Amazing Results of Positive Thinking* (New York: Simon & Schuster, 1959), 10.

Chapter 5: Recharge Your Batteries

1. Francis Gary Powers Jr., "The 1962 Spy Exchange of Powers for Abel," http://garypowers.org/1962-spy-exchange-of-powers-for-abel/.

2. Gail Blanke, *Throw Out Fifty Things: Clear the Clutter, Find Your Life* (New York: Grand Central Publishing, 2009).

3. Lee Strobel, *What Jesus Would Say: To Rush Limbaugh, Madonna, Bill Clinton, Michael Jordan, Bart Simpson, and You* (Grand Rapids: Zondervan, 1994), 27.

4. Bruce Allen Watson, *Exit Rommel: The Tunisian Campaign, 1942–43* (Mechanicsburg, PA: Stackpole Books, 1999), 132.

5. James E. Coté and Anton L. Allahar, *Generation on Hold: Coming of Age in the Late Twentieth Century* (New York: NY University Press, 1994), 62.

6. Anthony T. Evans, *Tony Evans' Book of Illustrations: Stories, Quotes, and Anecdotes from More than 30 Years of Preaching and Public Speaking* (Grand Rapids: Zondervan, 2009), 276–77.

7. Greg L. Hawkins and Cally Parkinson, *Follow Me* (Barrington, IL: The Willow Creek Association, 2008), 41.

8. John Maxwell, *Thinking for a Change: 11 Ways Highly Successful People Approach Life and Work* (New York: Warner Books, 2003), 27–33.

9. D. Martin Lloyd-Jones, *Spiritual Depression* (Grand Rapids: Eerdmans, 1965).

10. Adapted from James J. Lynch, *A Cry Unheard: New Insights into the Medical Consequences of Loneliness* (Baltimore: Bancroft Press, 2000).

11. Daniel Goleman, "Health: Psychology; Researchers Add Sounds of Silence to the Growing List of Health Risks," *New York Times*, August 4, 1988, http://www.nytimes.com/1988/08/04/us/health-psychology-researchers-add -sounds-silence-growing-list-health-risks.html. © 1988 The New York Times. All rights reserved. Used by permission and protected by the Copyright Laws of the United States. The printing, copying, redistribution,

or retransmission of this Content without express written permission is prohibited.

12. Adapted from John M. Gottman, *The Seven Principles for Making Marriage Work* (New York: Three Rivers Press, 1999).

13. Keld Jensen, "Intelligence Is Overrated: What You Really Need to Succeed," *Forbes*, April 12, 2012, http://www.forbes.com/sites/keldjensen/2012/04/12 /intelligence-is-overrated-what-you-really-need-to-succeed. From the Forbes Contributor Network and not necessarily the opinion of Forbes Media LLC. © 2012 Forbes. All rights reserved. Used by permission and protected by the Copyright Laws of the United States. The printing, copying, redistribution, or retransmission of this Content without express written permission is prohibited.

14. Thomas Joiner, *Lonely at the Top: The High Cost of Men's Success* (New York: St. Martin's Press, 2011).

15. Peter Foster, "Olympian from the Equator Wins at a Crawl," *The Telegraph*, September 20, 2000, http://www.telegraph.co.uk/news/worldnews /africaandindianocean /equatorialguinea/1356144/Olympian-from-the -Equator-wins-at-a-crawl.html. © Telegraph Media Group Limited 2000.

16. Several versions of this story exist. One possible early source is Dennis J. De Haan, "Ice Cream for the Soul," Our Daily Bread, February 22, 1999, http://odb .org/1999/02/22/ice-cream-for-the-soul/. Details as related here can be found in the version posted anonymously at Short Inspirational Writings and Inspiring Christian Stories, Inspirational Stories #3, http://gatewaytojesus.com /inspirationalstoriespage1.html.

Chapter 6: Raise Your Expectations

1. Walter Isaacson, *Steve Jobs* (New York: Simon & Schuster, 2011).

2. Ibid., 117.

3. Adapted from Adam Lashinsky, "Insights on the Writing of Steve Jobs," December 27, 2011, http://tech.fortune.cnn.com/2011/12/27/walter-isaacson -steve-jobs/, and Isaacson, *Steve Jobs*.

4. Glen Cole, personal conversation with the author. This conversation occurred over ten years ago; Pastor Cole has since passed away.

5. Halford E. Luccok, *Unfinished Business* (New York: Harper & Brothers, 1956), 54.

6. Mary Bellis, "Bad Predictions—Inventions that succeeded even though some important people stated otherwise," http://inventors.about.com/od/famous inventions/tp/bad-predictions.htm.

7. Ibid.

8. Ibid.

9. Joel Stonington, "Developing Space Tours and Car-Chargers," *Businessweek*,

November 9, 2010, http://www.businessweek.com/smallbiz/content/nov2010/sb2010119_961073.htm.

10. Jennifer Rosenberg, "The Stock Market Crash of 1929," http://history1900s.about.com/od/1920s/a/stockcrash1929.htm.

11. http://bible.org/illustration/quotes-48.

12. Loyola Marymount Athletics, "Roger Crawford to Receive 2013 ITA Achievement Award" (press release), September 4, 2013, http://www.lmulions.com/genrel/090413aaa.html.

13. Roger Crawford, *Think Again* (Roseville, CA: Thrive Publications, 2007), 193–95.

Chapter 7: Refocus on the Future

1. Berta Delgado, "Fruit of His Labors: His Big-Name Students Call Howard Hendricks a 'Prof' Like No Other," *Dallas Morning News*, January 4, 2003. Reprinted with permission of the *Dallas Morning News*.

2. Earl Palmer, Roberta Hestenes, and Howard Hendricks, *Mastering Teaching* (Colorado Springs: Multnomah, 1991), 75.

3. Dallas Theological Seminary, "The Life of Howard G. 'Prof' Hendricks," *DTS Magazine*, February 20, 2103, http://www.dts.edu/read/howard-hendricks-prof; Howard Hendricks and William Hendricks, *As Iron Sharpens Iron: Building Character in a Mentoring Relationship* (Chicago: Moody Press, 1999), 63.

4. Robert Fulghum, *All I Really Need to Know I Learned in Kindergarten* (New York: Random House, 1988).

5. Naresh Banera, "Case Study: Transforming Reuters," *Management Case Studies* (blog), August 18, 2011, http://managementgeneral.blogspot.com/2011/08/transforming-reuters.html.

6. Reggie Ogea, *The Daily Iberian* (New Iberia, LA), January 16, 1993, as quoted in "Sentence Sermons (Christian Inspiration) #106—Dreams (Meaning Goals)," http://garylchris.hubpages.com/hub/Sentence-Sermons-Christian-Inspiration-106-Dreams-Meaning-Goals.

7. Ibid.

Chapter 8: Play to Your Strengths

1. In 2011, the life expectancy in the United States was estimated by the World Bank to be 78.6 years (http://data.worldbank.org/indicator/SP.DYN.LE00.IN/countries/US--XS?display=graph), or 28,708 days.

2. Adapted from Billy Graham, *Just as I Am: The Autobiography of Billy Graham* (New York: HarperCollins, 2007).

3. Andrew Choi, *Soar on Wings Like the Eagle: Hope from the Garden of Eden to the End of the Island of Patmos* (Bloomington, IN: CrossBooks, 2011), 110.

4. Lisa Kepner, "Yates. Ira Griffith, Jr." *Handbook of Texas Online,* http://www.tshaonline.org/handbook/online/articles/fyazp. Published by the Texas State Historical Association.

5. Charles Swindoll, *Day by Day with Charles Swindoll* (Nashville: Thomas Nelson, 2000), 242.

6. Daily Mail Reporter, "Piece at last! Jigsaw fan, 86, finishes 5ft puzzle after SEVEN years," *Mail Online,* May 19, 2010, http://www.dailymail.co.uk/news/article-1279440/; Andrew Hough, "Pensioner's seven year jigsaw battle 'ends with one piece missing,'" *The Telegraph,* May 17, 2010, http://www.telegraph.co.uk/news/newstopics/howaboutthat/7730931, © Telegraph Media Group Limited 2010.

Chapter 9: Refuse to Go It Alone

1. Victoria Garshnek, "Soviet Space Flight: The Human Element," *Gravitational and Space Biology,* May 1988, http://gravitationalandspacebiology.org/index.php/journal/article/download/44/47.

2. Cass Werner Sperling, *Hollywood Be Thy Name: The Warner Brothers Story* (Lexington, KY: University Press of Kentucky, 1998), 326–27; "The Fall of the House of Warner: The Warner Brothers," *Bright Lights Film Journal* 82 (November 2013), http://brightlightsfilm.com/82/82-warner-brothers-bros-history.php#.Up_YX9OA 2Uk; Bob Thomas, *Clown Prince of Hollywood: The Antic Life and Times of Jack L. Warner* (New York: McGraw-Hill Publishing Company, 1990), 306.

3. Robert D. Putnam, *Bowling Alone: The Collapse and Revival of American Community* (New York: Touchstone Books, 2001), 332.

4. John Ortberg, "Every Life Needs a Cheering Section," sermon, Menlo Park Presbyterian Church, Menlo Park, CA, September 28, 2008.

5. Putnam, *Bowling Alone,* 331.

6. Harold Kushner, *When All You've Ever Wanted Isn't Enough: The Search for a Life That Matters* (New York: Simon & Schuster, 1986), 165–66.

7. Adapted from John Ortberg, *Love Beyond Reason* (Grand Rapids: Zondervan, 1998), 141–42.

8. Larry Crabb, *Connecting: Healing Ourselves and Our Relationships* (Nashville: Thomas Nelson, 1997), 150–51.

9. Ibid.

10. Brad Dupray, "Interview with Bryce Jessup." First published in *Christian Standard,* March 28, 2007, http://christianstandard.com/2007/03/interview-with-bryce-jessup-interview-and-photo-by-brad-dupray/.

11. Scot Giambalvo, "About Being Tremendous: An Interview with Charlie 'Tremendous' Jones," TremendousLifeBooks.com, October 16, 2008, http://tremendouslifebooks.org/tv/about-being-tremendous.

12. Ralph Waldo Emerson, *The Complete Works of Ralph Waldo Emerson*, vol. 2 (London: Bell & Daldy, 1866), 425.

13. Henrietta Mears, *What the Bible Is All About* (Ventura, CA: Regal Books from Gospel Light, 1953).

14. Henrietta C. Mears and Earl Roe, *Dream Big: The Henrietta Mears Story* (Ventura, CA: Regal Books from Gospel Light, 1990).

15. Ibid., 17.

16. S. Austin Allibone, comp., *Prose Quotations from Socrates to Macaulay* (1880), "Oliver Goldsmith Quotes," http://www.bartleby.com/349/authors/86.html.

17. Oswald Chambers, *My Utmost for His Highest* (Grand Rapids: Discovery House, 1963), 61. Taken from *My Utmost for His Highest* by Oswald Chambers, edited by James Reimann, © 1992 by Oswald Chambers Publications Assn., Ltd., and used by permission of Discovery House Publishers, Grand Rapids, MI 49501. All rights reserved.

18. Paul Tournier, *To Understand Each Other* (Louisville, KY: Westminster John Knox Press, 2000), 29.

19. Mike Morley, *300 Top Quotes to Help You in Any Situation* (Amazon Digital Services, 2012).

20. "Episode 15 China: Interview with Ambassador Winston Lord" (transcript), National Security Archive, http://www2.gwu.edu/~nsarchiv/coldwar/interviews/episode-15/lord1.html.

Chapter 10: Replace Burnout with Balance

1. Richard A. Swenson, MD, *Margin: Restoring Emotional, Physical, Financial, and Time Reserves to Overloaded Lives* (Colorado Springs: NavPress, 2004).

2. Ibid., 13.

3. "The Effects of Stress on Your Body," WebMD, July 23, 2012, http://www.webmd.com/mental-health/effects-of-stress-on-your-body.

4. Anne Fisher, "Your job might be killing you," CNNMoney, April 2, 2013, http://management.fortune.cnn.com/2013/04/02/work-stress-heart-disease/.

5. CIPD, "Stress is number one cause of long-term absence for the first time as job insecurity weighs heavy on the workplace, finds CIPD/Simplyhealth Absence survey" (press release), October 5, 2011, http://www.cipd.co.uk/pressoffice/press-releases/stress-number-one-cause-long.aspx.

6. National Sleep Foundation, "Annual Sleep in America Poll Exploring Connections with Communications Technology Use and Sleep" (press release), March 7, 2011, http://www.sleepfoundation.org/article/press-release

/annual-sleep-america-poll-exploring-connections-communications
-technology-use-.

7. Ibid.

8. Nancy Beach, "Heart Check," *Leadership* 22:1 (Winter 2001), 105ff.

9. F. John Reh, "Employee Benefits as a Management Tool," About.com
Management, http://management.about.com/cs/people/a/Benefits100198
.htm, quoting Brian G. Dyson, president and CEO, Coca-Cola Enterprises,
during his speech at the Georgia Tech Commencement, September 6, 1991.

10. Charles Swindoll, The Pastor's Soul Archive, The Pastor's Blog, http://
insightforliving.typepad.com/insight_for_living_blog/the_pastors_soul/.

11. Adapted from Rev. W. L. Gage, *Sabbath at Home*, Volume 3 (Boston, MA:
Rand, Avery, & Frye, 1869).

12. Charles Swindoll, *Growing Strong in the Seasons of Life* (Grand Rapids:
Zondervan, 1994), 213, as cited by http://www.sermonillustrations.com
/a-z/w/workaholic.htm.

Chapter 11: Play Great Defense

1. Phillip Yancey, *What's So Amazing About Grace?* (Grand Rapids: Zondervan,
1997), 85.

2. Gaylord Goertzen, "The Christian Leader," *Christianity Today* 35, no. 7
(February 26, 1991).

3. Warren W. Wiersbe, *The Wiersbe Bible Commentary: New Testament*
(Colorado Springs: David C. Cook, 2007), 24.

4. Ben Ferguson, *God, I've Got a Problem* (Ventura, CA: Regal Books,
1987), 59.

5. Corrie ten Boom, *Clippings from My Notebook* (Nashville: Thomas Nelson,
1982), 33.

6. Linda Dillow, *Calm My Anxious Heart* (Colorado Springs: NavPress, 2012),
116.

7. Bob P. Buford, *Game Plan: Winning Strategies for the Second Half of Your Life*
(Grand Rapids: Zondervan, 2009), 29.

8. Adam Silverstein, "UCLA's John Wooden, a legend in coaching and life,
passes away at age 99 (1910–2010)," Only Gators Get Out Alive, June 5,
2010, http://www.onlygators.com/06/05/2010/uclas-john-wooden-a
-legend-in-coaching-and-life-passes-away-at-age-99-1910-2010/.

9. Academy of Achievement, "Johnny Cash Interview," June 25, 1993, http://
www.achievement.org/autodoc/printmember/cas0int-1.

10. Mike Yaconelli was a lifelong friend until he passed away in 2003. He used
this expression many times.

11. "Edison Sees His Vast Plant Burn," *New York Times*, December 10, 1914, http://query.nytimes.com/mem/archive-free/pdf?res=F40614FF3F5C13738D DDA90994DA415B848DF1D3.
12. Glenn Van Ekeren, *The Speaker's Sourcebook: Quotes, Stories, and Anecdotes for Every Occasion* (Englewood Cliffs, NJ: Prentice Hall, 1988), 142–43.

Chapter 12: Unleashing Hope in Your Marriage

1. "Divorce in America Infographic," Daily Infographic, October 24, 2013, http://dailyinfographic.com/divorce-in-america-infographic.
2. Pastor Jack Smith, "Married to the Wrong Person?," sermon in the series Home Improvement, part 2 of 4, Elijah's Fire International Church, Elkhart, IN, www.efichurch.com.
3. Paul Tournier, *To Understand Each Other* (Louisville: Westminster John Knox Press, 2000), 13.
4. Paul Popenoe, *Marriage Is What You Make It* (St. Meinrad, IN: Abbey Press, 1970), 4.
5. Robert Fulghum, *It Was on Fire When I Lay Down on It* (New York: Random House, 2010), 160.
6. Gary Inrig, *True North* (Grand Rapids: Discovery House Publishers, 2002), 146–48.
7. Bob Benson, *Laughter in the Walls* (Nashville: Gaither Family Resources, 1996), 16–17.

Chapter 13: Unleashing Hope in Your Kids

1. Joke of the Week April-July 99, For the week of June 20, 1999, Fatherhood, http://www.humormatters.com/jokeof/jokeof99b.htm.
2. Ryan Johnson, "The Reality of Being a Teen Mom," TLC Parentables, Family Matters, June 28, 2011, http://parentables.howstuffworks.com/family -matters/reality-being-teen-mom.html.
3. Ibid.
4. National Abortion Federation, "Abortion Facts," http://www.prochoice.org /about_abortion/facts/teenage_women.html.
5. "11 Facts about Teens and STIs," DoSomething.org, http://www .dosomething.org/tipsandtools/11-facts-about-teens-and-stds.
6. Ibid.
7. "Teen Suicide Statistics," Statistic Brain, April 19, 2013, http://www .statisticbrain.com/teen-suicide-statistics/.
8. Ibid.

9. Children's Defense Fund, "Moments in America for Children," September 2013, http://www.childrensdefense.org/child-research-data-publications/moments-in-america-for-children.html.

10. Jean Potuchek, "Growing Older in a Youth-Obsessed Society," *Stepping into the Future* (blog), July 6, 2013, http://stepintofuture.wordpress.com/2013/07/06/growing-older-in-a-youth-obsessed-society/.

11. Marlene LeFever, "Children: The Church's Future," in PreachingToday.com, ed., *More Perfect Illustrations for Every Topic and Occasion* (Christianity Today International, 2003), 317.

12. "About Tony," Tony Campolo (website), June 10, 2013, http://tonycampolo.org/about-tony/.

13. Reprinted by permission of Angie K. Ward-Kucer.

Chapter 14: Unleashing Hope in Your Career

1. Kendra Gahagan, "Oldest Worker: At 100, Architect Still Aspires to Build Spires," *ABC News*, December 10, 2001, http://abcnews.go.com/Business/story?id=87500.

2. Chuck Norris, interview by Peter Lowe, Success 2000 Seminar (Dallas, TX), October 24, 2000.

Chapter 15: Unleashing Hope in Your Church

1. Adapted from David T. Olson, *The American Church in Crisis* (Grand Rapids: Zondervan, 2008).

2. Philip Yancey, *What's So Amazing About Grace?* (Grand Rapids: Zondervan, 1997), 11.

3. This version of the joke was popularized by Emo Philips on his album $E=mo^2$, although the general content of the joke likely predates him.

Chapter 16: Unleashing Hope in Your Community

1. Robert D. Dáliva (staff), "Editorial: Building on Bishop Carthen's legacy is the challenge we now face," *Sacramento Bee*, September 27, 2013, http://www.sacbee.com/2013/09/27/5772117/editorial-building-on-bishop-carthens.html#mi_rss=Editorials. © 2013 McClatchy. All rights reserved. Used by permission and protected by the Copyright Laws of the United States. The printing, copying, redistribution, or retransmission of this Content without express written permission is prohibited.

2. Robert D. Dávila, "Bishop Sherwood Carthen, 54, was influential church and community leader," *Sacramento Bee*, October 1, 2013, http://www.sacbee.com/2013/09/25/5769142/bishop-sherwood-carthen-54-was.html. © 2013 McClatchy. All rights reserved. Used by permission and protected by

the Copyright Laws of the United States. The printing, copying, redistribution, or retransmission of this Content without express written permission is prohibited.

3. Ibid.

Chapter 17: Unleashing Hope in the World

1. Adapted from many retellings of the story by Loren Eiseley: Loren Eiseley, *The Star Thrower* (Boston: Mariner Books, 1979), 169.

2. Adapted from John Ortberg, *If You Want to Walk on Water You've Got to Get Out of the Boat* (Grand Rapids: Zondervan, 2001), 89–90.

3. See more of Pastor Kim's story on YouTube: http://www.youtube.com/watch?v=98lHTOc0D60.

4. From a video the author viewed at the Compassion International banquet on October 8, 2011.

ABOUT THE AUTHOR

Ray Johnston has a rich and varied background as a university and graduate-school professor, speaker, writer, and founder of Thrive Communications. A veteran of youth and adult ministries as a national speaker for Youth Specialties, Ray is also the founder of Thriving Churches International. Each year his Thrive Leadership Conference sells out months in advance, with more than four thousand leaders attending from across the country and around the world. He is the founding pastor of Bayside Church, which he describes as "a church for people who don't like church." Bayside has grown into one of the largest churches in the nation, with more than twelve thousand people coming together every weekend at the Granite Bay campus and thousands more in multiple churches throughout the Sacramento region. Ray has spoken to more than four million people over the last ten years and serves on the board of trustees at Azusa Pacific University, where he graduated. Ray and his wife, Carol, have four children.

RECHARGE
REFRESH
RENEW

THRIVE ⟫⟫⟫
CONFERENCE

THRIVECONFERENCE.ORG

4 FACTS

1 The American Church Is in Crisis—It's Been Declining for Decades.

2 Americans Like Jesus a Whole Lot More than They Like Christians.

3 The Church Is Losing the Next Generation.

4 All of This Could Be Turned Around! Maybe the American Church Needs to Take a Good Look at Getting Reconnected to Its Founder.

Join the discussion at
REINTRODUCINGJESUS.COM